Naturopathy

The Essence of Naturopathy and Pranic Healing

(Evolve to the Alternate Form of Naturopathic Medicine for a Healthier)

Manuel Bolton

Published By **Elena Holly**

Manuel Bolton

Naturopathy: The Essence of Naturopathy and Pranic Healing (Evolve to the Alternate Form of Naturopathic Medicine for a Healthier)

ISBN 978-1-9990334-7-7

No part of this guidebook shall be reproduced in any form without permission in writing from the publisher except in the case of brief quotations embodied in critical articles or reviews.

Legal & Disclaimer

The information contained in this book is not designed to replace or take the place of any form of medicine or professional medical advice. The information in this book has been provided for educational & entertainment purposes only.

The information contained in this book has been compiled from sources deemed reliable, and it is accurate to the best of the Author's knowledge; however, the Author cannot guarantee its accuracy and validity and cannot be held liable for any errors or omissions. Changes are periodically made to this book. You must consult your doctor or get professional medical advice before using any of the suggested remedies, techniques, or information in this book.

Upon using the information contained in this book, you agree to hold harmless the Author from and against any damages, costs, and expenses, including any legal fees potentially resulting from the application of any of the information provided by this guide. This disclaimer applies to any damages or injury caused by the use and application, whether directly or indirectly, of any advice or information presented, whether for breach of contract, tort, negligence, personal injury, criminal intent, or under any other cause of action.

You agree to accept all risks of using the information presented inside this book. You need to consult a professional medical practitioner in order to ensure you are both able and healthy enough to participate in this program.

Table Of Contents

Chapter 1: Understanding Detoxification In Naturopathy

The technological understanding behind cleansing

Detoxi cation is a natural machine that takes area inside the body every day. It is the approach of getting rid of pollutants from the body through diverse organs collectively with the liver, kidneys, lungs, and pores and pores and skin. However, due to the increasing publicity to pollutants, chemical materials, and awful way of life conduct, our our our bodies might not be capable of preserve up with the detoxi cation way. This can lead to the accumulation of pollutants inside the frame, that might reason numerous fitness problems.

The technological knowledge behind detoxi cation consists of data how the body receives rid of pollutants and the function of numerous organs in this approach. The liver is the number one detoxi action organ within the frame. It is responsible for converting pollutants into lots awful lot much less dangerous materials that may be eliminated from the frame. The kidneys additionally play a crucial function in detoxi cation with the aid of ltering out waste merchandise from the blood and eliminating them through urine.

The lungs take away pollution through respiratory, at the same time because the pores and skin receives rid of pollutants via sweating. The lymphatic device, that could be a network of vessels and tissues, furthermore permits in detoxi cation through using getting rid of waste products from the body and transporting them to the liver for processing.

Various natural recovery approaches can assist the frame's natural detoxi cation method. One such remedy is fasting, which lets in the body to cognizance on casting off pollution in location of digesting food. Another treatment is the usage of herbs which includes milk thistle, dandelion, and turmeric, that could resource liver function and useful resource in detoxi cation. Detoxi cation diets that focus on whole meals, end result, and vegetables also can assist the frame's natural detoxi cation manner. Such diets provide essential nutrients that assist inside the elimination of pollution from the body.

In stop, the technology in the back of detoxi cation involves data how the frame removes pollutants and the function of severa organs on this process. Natural remedies such as fasting, herbs, and detox diets can assist the frame's natural detoxi cation way and sell widespread health and well-being. It is important to are trying to find recommendation from a naturopathic clinical medical health practitioner in advance than embarking on any detoxi cation software program to make certain that it is steady and e ective on your person dreams.

The unique varieties of pollutants and their effects at the frame

The di erent kinds of pollutants and their e ects at the frame

Toxins are harmful substances that can negatively a ect our fitness and nicely-being. They can come from loads of sources, which consist of the meals we devour, the air we breathe, and the goods we use. In naturopathy, detoxi cation is an critical manner that allows the frame put off those pollution and repair stability. Here are a number of the di erent forms of pollutants and their e ects on the frame.

Environmental pollutants

Environmental pollutants are materials which is probably determined in our surroundings, which include pollution, insecticides, and heavy metals. These pollutants can cause a number of health issues, in conjunction with breathing problems, neurological problems, and most cancers. They can also a ect our immune tool, making us extra susceptible to infections and ailments.

Food pollution

Food pollutants are materials which is probably found in the meals we consume, which embody insecticides, preservatives, and additives. These pollution can motive digestive problems, in ammation, and hormonal imbalances. They can also a ect our energy levels and highbrow readability.

Mold pollutants

Mold pollution are produced with the aid of using fine sorts of mold which can expand in damp environments, collectively with basements and toilets. These pollution can purpose breathing troubles, allergic reactions, and neurological problems. They also can a ect our immune gadget, making us greater liable to infections and ailments.

Heavy metallic pollution

Heavy metal pollutants are substances which can be determined in the environment, such as lead, mercury, and arsenic. These pollution can gather inside the body over time and reason numerous fitness issues, along side neurological troubles, cognitive decline, and most cancers. They also can a ect our immune device, making us greater liable to infections and illnesses.

Chemical pollutants

Chemical pollutants are substances which is probably determined in products we use each day, collectively with cleaning merchandise, private care products, and plastics. These pollution can cause hormonal imbalances, reproductive troubles, and maximum cancers. They also can a ect our immune device, making us more susceptible to infections and ailments. In end, pollutants must have a extensive form of horrible e ects on our fitness and properly-being. In naturopathy, detoxi cation is an important approach that lets in the body eliminate the ones pollutants and restore balance. By understanding the di erent varieties of pollutants and their e ects on the body, we're capable of take steps to lessen our exposure and improve our typical health.

The feature of the liver in cleaning

The liver is an important organ of the human body that plays a critical role in detoxi cation. It is answerable for breaking down pollution, pills, and alcohol, and getting rid of them from the frame. The liver moreover produces bile, which facilitates within the digestion of fat and absorbs fat-soluble vitamins. It performs a crucial function in retaining the body's everyday health.

One of the primary abilties of the liver is detoxi cation. The liver detoxi es the frame with the beneficial resource of processing and doing away with pollution. The liver cells, furthermore known as hepatocytes, include enzymes that damage down pollutants and convert them into an awful lot much less dangerous substances. These materials are then eliminated from the body thru urine or feces.

The liver detoxi es both endogenous and exogenous pollution. Endogenous pollution are produced in the frame, together with ammonia, it truly is a byproduct of protein metabolism. Exogenous pollution are outside pollution that input the body through meals, water, air, and one-of-a-type assets. Examples of exogenous pollutants encompass pesticides, heavy metals, alcohol, and tablets.

The liver detoxi es these pollution in two levels. In Phase I, the liver breaks down the pollution into intermediate compounds the use of enzymes collectively with cytochrome P450. In Phase II, the intermediate compounds are further broken down into water-soluble materials that may be eliminated from the frame.

The liver furthermore detoxi es capsules and medicines. When a person takes treatment, the liver tactics it and gets rid of it from the body. If the liver isn't always functioning efficiently, the medication can gather within the frame, primary to toxicity.

The liver plays a vital function in preserving general fitness. A wholesome liver can assist decorate digestion, increase immunity, and increase power tiers. However, a liver this is overloaded with pollution can motive severa health troubles together with fatigue, digestive troubles, and pores and skin troubles. Therefore, it's miles vital to maintain liver health via detoxi cation.

In naturopathy, detoxi cation is a natural way to cleanse the liver and put off pollution from the frame. A naturopathic detox utility may additionally moreover encompass nutritional modifications, natural dietary nutritional supplements, and lifestyle modi cations. It is essential to consult a quali ed naturopath in advance than starting a detox software program to make sure it is solid and e ective.

Detoxification for Weight Loss in Naturopathy

The link amongst pollution and weight gain

As we keep to live in a worldwide whole of pollution, it is vital to recognize the link among pollutants and weight advantage. Toxins are volatile materials that can enter our our our bodies through the air we breathe, the food we consume, and the goods we use. These pollutants can impair our body's herbal functionality to detoxify, fundamental to quite a number fitness problems, collectively with weight gain.

Toxins can a ect the body's metabolism, hormones, and digestion. When pollution input the body, they are able to disrupt the endocrine tool, this is accountable for regulating hormones. This disruption can bring about insulin resistance and an increase inside the strain hormone cortisol, each of which could make contributions to weight gain.

Furthermore, pollutants can also a ect the liver, this is the frame's primary organ for detoxi cation. When the liver is overloaded with pollution, it may grow to be slow and not capable of well way and do away with waste from the frame. This can result in the buildup of pollutants within the fats cells, which can make a contribution to weight gain.

Moreover, pollutants also can a ect the digestion way. When we eat a diet plan excessive in processed meals and pollutants, our digestive device can end up in amed, leading to a situation known as leaky gut syndrome. This scenario allows pollutants to leak into the bloodstream, causing in ammation at some point of the body, which include in fats cells. This in ammation can cause weight advantage and di culty dropping weight. In cease, the link among pollutants and weight advantage is signi cant. Toxins can disrupt the body's herbal techniques, main to weight advantage and di culty dropping weight. Detoxi cation is crucial to assist the frame in getting rid of pollution and restoring critical fitness. Through a complete approach to herbal recuperation, together with detoxi cation in naturopathy, we are able to accumulate simplest weight, strength, and electricity.

Foods and dietary supplements that aid in weight loss

Weight loss is a not unusual cause for masses people, and at the same time as there are various diets and weight reduction programs handy, some people pick to take a extra natural and holistic technique. In naturopathy, there are various substances and dietary supplements that would useful resource in weight reduction even as additionally promoting regular fitness and well-being.

1. Green tea

Green tea is a famous beverage this is wealthy in antioxidants and has been hooked up to useful useful resource in weight loss. The ca eine and catechins in green tea can help decorate metabolism and boom fats burning, making it a exquisite addition to any weight-reduction plan.

2. Probiotics

Probiotics are bene cial bacteria that live in the gut and assist to help digestion and normal health. Studies have confirmed that probiotics may also moreover beneficial resource in weight loss through reducing in ammation and enhancing insulin sensitivity.

3. Fiber-wealthy meals

Fiber is an vital nutrient that could help to sell emotions of fullness and reduce calorie consumption. Foods which may be immoderate in her encompass fruits, vegetables, entire grains, and legumes. Adding the ones meals to your diet regime will let you feel more satis ed and decrease the chance of overeating.

4. Protein-wealthy meals

Protein is a few different critical nutrient that can help to promote feelings of fullness and decrease calorie intake. Foods which might be excessive in protein encompass lean meats, sh, eggs, and dairy products. Adding those substances on your diet plan let you feel more satis ed and decrease the chance of overeating.

5. Apple cider vinegar

Apple cider vinegar is a well-known supplement that has been confirmed to useful useful resource in weight loss. The acetic acid in apple cider vinegar can help to lessen urge for food and growth feelings of fullness, making it much less complex to stick to a weight loss plan.

6. Chromium

Chromium is a mineral that might help to adjust blood sugar ranges and reduce cravings for sugary elements. Supplementing with chromium also can assist to promote weight reduction and decorate ordinary health.

Incorporating these materials and nutritional supplements into your diet can help to aid weight loss at the same time as also promoting fashionable fitness and properly-being. It's essential to take into account that at the same time as these substances and nutritional supplements can be useful; they ought to be used alongside aspect a healthful weight loss plan and way of lifestyles for fine results. Consult with a naturopathic medical physician or healthcare professional before beginning any new complement every day.

Exercise and detoxing

Exercise is one of the most e ective techniques to help your body's natural detoxi cation methods. When you exercising, your frame produces sweat, which lets in to eliminate pollution through your skin additionally, exercising will increase blood

ow and oxygenation, which enables to ush pollutants out of your organs and tissues. Regular exercising also helps wholesome digestion, it definitely is vital for putting off waste and pollutants from your body.

There are many di erent varieties of workout that may assist detoxi cation in naturopathy. Cardiovascular exercising, which consist of going for walks, cycling, or swimming, can help to increase your coronary heart price and raise drift, which could enhance your body's capability to cast off pollutants. Strength schooling bodily sports, which incorporate weight lifting or body weight physical video video games, can help to assemble muscle companies, which can enhance your metabolism and help wholesome detoxi cation.

Yoga and other thoughts-frame sporting sports additionally can be bene cial for detoxi cation in naturopathy. These varieties of physical sports activities can assist to reduce stress, that might enhance your frame's capability to detoxify. Yoga and distinct mind-frame sporting sports can also enhance your digestion and guide wholesome elimination, that is critical for detoxi cation.

Incorporating exercise into your every day recurring may be tough, however it's miles essential to nd a sort of exercising which you revel in and that ts into some time table. Aim to exercising for at least 30 minutes regular with day, ve days in keeping with week. You can also consist of special wholesome conduct into your normal, in conjunction with eating a balanced eating regimen, staying hydrated, and getting enough sleep, to manual your body's herbal detoxi cation strategies.

If you're new to work out, it's miles vital to start slowly and grade by grade boom the depth and period of your sporting activities. Consult with a quali ed naturopathic medical doctor or private instructor to growth a stable and e ective exercising plan it clearly is custom designed in your precise dreams and desires.

In conclusion, workout is an essential element of naturopathic detoxi cation. Regular exercising can help to aid healthful circulate, digestion, and removal, which is probably all crucial for removing pollutants from your frame. By incorporating workout into your each day every day, you could beneficial useful resource your body's natural detoxi cation strategies and revel in stepped forward health and electricity.

Chapter 2: Liver Health In Naturopathy

The function of the liver in cleansing

The liver is one of the maximum critical organs in the human frame, and it plays a crucial function in detoxi cation. The liver is answerable for processing and ltering pollutants from the blood, generating bile, and breaking down fats and proteins.

The liver detoxi cation approach involves ranges: Phase I and Phase II. In Phase I, the liver breaks down pollution into smaller, less dangerous molecules. This way consists of enzymes that redesign pollution into intermediate compounds that are then despatched to Phase II for similarly cleansing processing.

In Phase II, the liver combines the intermediate compounds with exceptional molecules to cause them to water-soluble, allowing them to be excreted from the body. This method consists of pretty a few enzymes, which include glutathione, sulfation, glucuronidation, and methylation.

If the liver is overwhelmed with pollution or no longer functioning well, pollution can increase inside the body, major to an entire lot of fitness issues. This is why it's far important to manual liver fitness through detoxi cation.

There are many natural tactics to manual liver detoxi cation, together with nutritional adjustments, nutritional dietary supplements, and lifestyle modi cations. Eating a healthy, whole substances weight loss program that is wealthy in end result and veggies can provide the liver with the vitamins it desires to characteristic optimally.

Certain dietary dietary supplements, together with milk thistle, dandelion root, and turmeric, also can assist liver health and detoxi cation. Lifestyle modi cations, which consist of lowering alcohol consumption, quitting smoking, and reducing exposure to environmental pollution, also can assist resource liver feature.

Detoxi cation is important for famous health and nicely being, and the liver performs a vital function in this technique. By supporting liver health via natural strategies, human beings can promote gold preferred detoxi cation and enhance their commonplace fitness and strength.

Foods and dietary supplements that promote liver health

The liver is one of the most crucial organs in our frame, accountable for severa capabilities, including detoxi cation, metabolism, and protein synthesis. However, due to our every day publicity to pollutants and horrible manner of existence conduct, the liver can become overworked and broken, maximum crucial to numerous health issues. Therefore, it's miles vital to guide liver health through a healthy weight loss plan and nutritional supplements.

Here are a few meals and dietary nutritional dietary supplements which can promote liver health:

1. Leafy Greens: Spinach, kale, and different leafy veggies are rich in antioxidants and chlorophyll, which could help to detoxify the liver and decrease in ammation.

2. Cruciferous Vegetables: Broccoli, cauli ower, and Brussels sprouts include compounds that guide liver detoxi cation and protect in competition to liver harm.

three. Garlic: Garlic consists of sulfur compounds that might activate liver enzymes and ush out pollutants from the body.

four. Turmeric: Turmeric consists of curcumin, a powerful anti-in ammatory and antioxidant that could protect toward liver damage and sell liver regeneration.

5. Milk Thistle: Milk thistle is a herb that has been used for hundreds of years to assist liver health. It consists of a compound known as silymarin, which can guard liver cells from harm and improve liver characteristic.

6. Dandelion Root: Dandelion root is a natural diuretic that would assist to ush out

pollutants from the liver and beautify liver feature.

7. N-acetyl Cysteine (NAC): NAC is an amino acid which could increase degrees of the antioxidant glutathione in the body, which could defend towards liver damage.

eight. Vitamin E: Vitamin E is an antioxidant that could guard liver cells from oxidative harm and enhance liver function.

9. Omega-three Fatty Acids: Omega-three fatty acids can reduce in ammation and protect in competition to liver damage.

It is vital to phrase that at the same time as those meals and nutritional nutritional supplements can aid liver health, they need to now not be used as an alternative for clinical treatment. If you accept as true with you studied you have got liver issues or exceptional fitness issues, communicate with a quali ed healthcare practitioner in advance than starting any new dietary dietary dietary supplements or dietary adjustments.

In give up, incorporating those liver-supporting ingredients and nutritional dietary supplements into your diet can assist to sell liver health and frequently taking place nicely-being. A healthful liver is critical for most excellent fitness, and by way of the usage of way of looking after it, you can beautify your high-quality of existence and prevent future health troubles.

Lifestyle changes for liver fitness

Lifestyle adjustments for liver health are crucial for absolutely everyone who desires to revel in natural healing. The liver is one of the most crucial organs in the frame, responsible for ltering pollution and waste merchandise from the bloodstream. When the liver is overloaded with pollutants, it is able to come to be broken and much much less e ective at performing its important skills.

To hold highest remarkable liver fitness, it's far crucial to make sure way of life changes. Here are some steps you may take:

1. Reduce your alcohol intake

Alcohol is a primary stressor on the liver, and immoderate consumption can cause quite a number of liver troubles. Cut again in your alcohol consumption, and keep away from binge ingesting.

2. Eat a wholesome food plan

A healthy food regimen is crucial for liver health. Focus on consuming loads of fruits and greens, lean protein, and healthy fats. Avoid processed elements, sugary liquids, and excessive-fat food.

3. Maintain a healthful weight

Obesity is a high threat factor for liver disorder. If you're obese, art work on dropping weight thru a combination of wholesome ingesting and exercising.

4. Exercise frequently

Exercise is vital for not unusual fitness, and it may moreover help enhance liver function.

Aim for at the least half of of-hour of mild workout most days of the week.

five. Avoid pollution

Toxins are a number one burden on the liver. Avoid exposure to environmental pollution which incorporates insecticides and chemical substances, and choose natural cleansing products and personal care merchandise rather.

6. Stay hydrated

Dehydration could make it greater di cult for the liver to feature nicely. Drink masses of water at a few stage within the day to live hydrated.

By making the ones way of existence modifications, you can assist assist your liver fitness and promote herbal restoration. Combining those modifications with special natural detoxi cation strategies can help you obtain nice fitness and nicely being.

Detoxification for Skin Health in Naturopathy

How pollution affect the pores and skin

Toxins are observed in our environment, meals, and household merchandise. They could have a devastating e ect on our health, at the side of our pores and pores and pores and skin. The pores and pores and skin is the most vital organ in the frame and is liable for protective us from outdoor elements. When pollution accumulate in the frame, they could purpose a number of skin issues which consist of acne, rosacea, eczema, and psoriasis.

Toxins can enter the frame via severa method, at the side of the meals we eat, the air we breathe, and the products we use. Chemicals decided in processed meals, insecticides, and pollution within the air can all make a contribution to toxic overload in the frame. These pollutants can then accumulate inside the liver, this is liable for detoxifying the frame, and may purpose pores and skin issues.

One way wherein pollutants a ect the pores and pores and skin is through the use of disrupting the herbal balance of the pores and pores and skin's microbiome. The microbiome is a group of micro organism, fungi, and wonderful microorganisms that stay at the pores and pores and pores and skin. These microorganisms play a critical characteristic in protective the pores and pores and skin and preventing infections. When pollution disrupt the microbiome, it is able to reason an overgrowth of risky micro organism, that can purpose pores and pores and skin problems which incorporates acne and eczema.

Toxins can also motive in ammation within the body, that may bring about skin troubles. In ammation is the frame's herbal response to harm or infection. When pollution acquire inside the frame, they might motive persistent in ammation, which could cause pretty a few health problems, collectively with pores and pores and pores and skin problems.

In addition to disrupting the microbiome and causing in ammation, pollution can also damage the pores and pores and pores and skin's collagen and elastin bers. Collagen and elastin are proteins that offer the pores and skin its shape and elasticity. When those bers are damaged, the skin can emerge as saggy and wrinkled.

To avoid the bad e ects of pollutants on the pores and pores and skin, it is essential to detoxify the body frequently. This may be finished thru a healthful diet regime, regular workout, and the use of herbal merchandise. Eating a healthy eating plan rich in end result, veggies, and entire grains can assist to assist the liver's detoxi cation method. Exercise allows to improve flow, that may help to do away with pollutants from the body. And using herbal merchandise, free from dangerous chemical substances, can assist to guide the pores and skin's natural stability.

In end, pollution ought to have a signi cant impact at the pores and skin. To preserve healthy pores and pores and skin, it's miles crucial to detoxify the frame regularly and keep away from exposure to risky chemical substances. By doing so, we can help the body's herbal detoxi cation techniques and preserve a healthful, glowing complexion.

Chapter 3: Foods And Supplements

Your pores and pores and pores and skin is an indication of your generic health. Therefore, it is essential to take well care of your pores and pores and pores and skin with the resource of ingesting the right food and dietary dietary dietary supplements that promote healthy pores and pores and skin. Here are some ingredients and nutritional dietary supplements which you ought to keep in mind which includes on your healthy eating plan to promote healthful skin.

1. Omega-three Fatty Acids

Omega-3 fatty acids, determined in sh like salmon, sardines, and mackerel, are critical for healthful pores and skin. They help lessen in ammation, which can motive redness and zits. Omega-3s moreover help keep your pores and skin hydrated and supple.

2. Vitamin C

Vitamin C is a amazing antioxidant that lets in guard your pores and pores and skin from damage because of free radicals. It stimulates collagen manufacturing, which permits preserve your skin rm and elastic. You can nd nutrition C in citrus stop result, strawberries, and kiwis.

three. Vitamin E

Vitamin E is every different antioxidant that helps protect your pores and skin from damage due to unfastened radicals. It also enables reduce in ammation and enhance pores and pores and pores and skin texture. You can nd diet E in nuts, seeds, and leafy green greens.

four. Zinc

Zinc is an important mineral that allows alter the manufacturing of oil for your pores and pores and skin. It moreover allows heal wounds and decrease in ammation. You can nd zinc in meat, seafood, and legumes.

5. Probiotics

Probiotics are unique micro organism that help hold the stableness of your intestine microbiome. A healthy intestine microbiome is essential for wholesome pores and skin. Probiotics may be determined in fermented meals like yogurt, ke r, and sauerkraut.

6. Collagen

Collagen is a protein that lets in preserve your skin rm and elastic. As you age, your frame produces loads tons less collagen, that can lead to wrinkles and sagging pores and pores and pores and skin. You can nd collagen in bone broth, collagen supplements, and a few skincare products.

In give up, consuming the proper factors and nutritional supplements is crucial for selling healthy pores and skin. Incorporating these meals and dietary dietary supplements into your healthy dietweight-reduction plan can help lessen in ammation, improve pores and pores and skin texture, and maintain your pores and pores and pores and skin hydrated and supple. Remember to seek advice from a naturopathic scientific medical doctor in advance than beginning any new supplement recurring.

Natural treatments for common pores and pores and pores and skin situations

Natural remedies for commonplace pores and pores and skin situations

Skin situations are some of the maximum not unusual health issues people face. From acne to eczema, those situations cannot most effective be nerve-racking however additionally take a toll on one's arrogance. While there are numerous over-the-counter and prescription medicinal tablets to be had, herbal treatments additionally can be e ective in treating pores and pores and skin situations. Here are some herbal remedies for commonplace pores and pores and skin situations:

1. Tea tree oil for pimples: Tea tree oil has antiseptic properties which could help lessen zits-causing micro organism. Mix a few drops

of tea tree oil with a issuer oil like coconut oil and apply it to the a ected location.

2. Aloe vera for sunburn: Aloe vera has anti-in ammatory homes that could help soothe sunburned pores and skin. Apply aloe vera gel proper away to the a ected area for treatment.

3. Chamomile for eczema: Chamomile has anti-in ammatory and antibacterial residences that might assist reduce the in ammation and itchiness associated with eczema. Brew chamomile tea and use a cotton ball to use it to the a ected place.

4. Honey for dry pores and skin: Honey has moisturizing houses that could assist hydrate dry pores and skin. Apply uncooked honey straight away to the a ected location and allow it take a seat down for 15-20 mins in advance than rinsing o .

five. Oatmeal for itching: Oatmeal has anti-in ammatory homes that could help lessen itching. Mix oatmeal with water to form a thick paste and use it on the a ected area for comfort.

6. Apple cider vinegar for dandru : Apple cider vinegar has antifungal houses that would assist reduce dandru . Mix equal parts apple cider vinegar and water and apply it to the scalp. Let it sit for a few minutes earlier than rinsing o .

7. Turmeric for psoriasis: Turmeric has anti-in ammatory residences that could help lessen the in ammation related to psoriasis. Mix turmeric with water to shape a paste and use it on the a ected vicinity.

These herbal remedies may be e ective in treating commonplace pores and pores and skin situations. However, it is crucial to go to a healthcare expert before attempting any new treatments, in particular if you have a clinical circumstance or are taking remedy.

Detoxification for Energy and Vitality in Naturopathy

How pollutants have an impact on power levels

Toxins can be determined anywhere, in conjunction with the food we consume, the air we breathe, and the products we use. These pollutants can collect in our frame and a ect our preferred health, on the side of our electricity tiers. In this subchapter, we'll discover how pollutants a ect our electricity levels and what we can do to detoxify our body and increase our strength.

Toxins can a ect our energy levels in severa methods. Firstly, they are able to harm our cells and impair their capacity to supply power. Secondly, they might intrude with the functioning of our organs, particularly the liver, which plays a important characteristic in detoxi cation. When the liver is overloaded with pollution, it may't feature properly, essential to fatigue and distinct health troubles. Thirdly, pollutants also can a ect our hormones, which regulate our strength degrees. When our hormones are imbalanced, we may additionally enjoy fatigue and wonderful signs.

Detoxi cation is a herbal machine that our body undergoes to take away pollution and waste products. However, on the equal time as our body is overloaded with pollutants, it couldn't be capable of preserve up with the demand. This is wherein detoxi cation in naturopathy is available in. Naturopathy is a holistic approach to health that makes a speciality of herbal treatments and way of existence changes to manual the frame's herbal healing system. Detoxi cation in naturopathy includes a combination of nutritional and manner of lifestyles changes, further to herbal remedies to manual the body's detoxi cation approach. For example, a detox weight loss plan can also additionally consist of casting off processed elements, sugar, ca eine, alcohol, and special pollutants out of your weight-reduction plan, and converting them with nutrient-dense complete components, which incorporates culmination, veggies, whole grains, and lean proteins.

In addition to dietary adjustments, naturopathy additionally recommends life-style changes, collectively with getting sufficient sleep, lowering pressure, and engaging in ordinary physical interest. These lifestyle changes can assist reduce the burden on our liver and help our body's herbal detoxi cation manner.

Natural remedies, together with herbs, dietary dietary dietary supplements, and important oils, can also be used to manual the body's detoxi cation manner. For example, milk thistle is a herb that has been shown to guide liver health and detoxi cation. Ginger, turmeric, and garlic also are natural treatments which have detoxifying homes.

In give up, pollutants also can have a awful impact on our power ranges, however with the assist of detoxi cation in naturopathy, we will aid our body's natural recuperation way and increase our electricity. By making dietary and manner of lifestyles modifications, and using herbal treatments, we're able to lessen the weight on our liver and manual our frame's herbal detoxi cation gadget.

Foods and dietary supplements that promote electricity and energy

When it entails maintaining a wholesome body and thoughts, strength and energy are key elements. But with the hustle and bustle of every day lifestyles, it could be hard to hold maximum appropriate electricity levels in some unspecified time in the future of the day. Fortunately, there are numerous materials and dietary dietary supplements that would assist sell electricity and electricity definitely.

One of the best methods to enhance strength and energy is thru consuming nutrient-dense meals which might be immoderate in vitamins, minerals, and antioxidants. Some of the tremendous meals for energy and energy include:

Leafy veggies: Greens like spinach, kale, and collard vegetables are immoderate in iron, it's vital for oxygen transport and electricity manufacturing.

Nuts and seeds: Nuts and seeds are excessive in wholesome fat, protein, and ber, which assist keep you feeling complete and energized in some unspecified time within the destiny of the day.

Whole grains: Whole grains like brown rice, quinoa, and oats are high in complicated carbohydrates, which provide sustained energy and help regulate blood sugar stages.

Berries: Berries like blueberries, strawberries, and raspberries are excessive in antioxidants, which protect in opposition to cellular harm and promote ordinary fitness and energy.

In addition to the ones substances, there also are many nutritional supplements that might assist boom energy and electricity. Some of the superb dietary dietary dietary supplements for power and electricity embody:

Vitamin B12: B12 is essential for electricity manufacturing and may help reduce fatigue and enhance highbrow readability.

CoQ10: CoQ10 is an antioxidant that performs a key function in power manufacturing and can help enhance patience and reduce fatigue.

Ashwagandha: Ashwagandha is an adaptogenic herb that lets in the body deal with pressure and decorate electricity ranges.

Maca: Maca is a root vegetable that is excessive in nutrients, minerals, and antioxidants, and can assist decorate electricity, temper, and familiar energy.

By incorporating these ingredients and nutritional dietary dietary supplements into your each day every day, you may help promote energy and power glaringly and manual you're not unusual fitness and nicely-being.

Chapter 4: Lifestyle Adjustments For Accelerated Strength

Feeling worn-out and gradual is a commonplace grievance in present day rapid-paced global. Many people turn to ca eine and sugary snacks to enhance their energy stages; however those quick xes only provide a brief answer. To truely boom your energy degrees, it is crucial to make manner of lifestyles modifications that assist your frame's herbal rhythms and promote general fitness. Here are a few pointers for reinforcing your strength manifestly:

1. Get Enough Sleep

Your body needs pinnacle sufficient relaxation to function well, and sleep is important for keeping electricity levels. Aim for seven to 9 hours of sleep every night time, and try to set up a ordinary sleep time table to help adjust your frame's natural sleepwake cycle.

2. Exercise Regularly

Physical hobby is an amazing way to decorate energy ranges. Exercise will increase go with the flow and oxygen ow to the body, which permits to beautify strength and temper. Aim for at least half of-hour of moderate exercising every day, which embody brisk strolling, cycling, or swimming.

3. Eat a Balanced Diet

The meals you eat has a right away impact to your energy levels. Focus on ingesting a balanced food regimen that consists of plenty of sparkling cease result and greens, complete grains, lean protein, and healthful fat. Avoid processed components, sugary snacks, and immoderate ca eine and alcohol, that would all make a contribution to fatigue and coffee power tiers.

4. Stay Hydrated

Dehydration can make contributions to feelings of fatigue and coffee electricity tiers. Make sure to drink loads of water sooner or later of the day, and keep away from sugary drinks and excessive ca eine, that might dehydrate the frame.

5. Manage Stress

Stress can take a toll on your frame and contribute to fatigue and low electricity ranges. Practice stress-decreasing strategies which includes meditation, yoga, or deep respiratory sports activities activities to help control pressure and promote rest.

By making those smooth way of life changes, you may boom your power ranges manifestly and promote popular health and well-being. Incorporate the ones hints into your each day regular and enjoy the bene ts of multiplied power and electricity.

Detoxification for Hormonal Balance in Naturopathy

The hyperlink among pollution and hormonal imbalances

Toxins are one of the essential reasons of hormonal imbalances within the frame.

Hormonal imbalances can motive a whole lot of health issues, together with weight gain, fatigue, mood swings, or perhaps infertility. Understanding the hyperlink among pollution and hormonal imbalances is vital to reaching most effective health and well-being.

The human frame is uncovered to pollutants on a each day foundation. These pollution come from an entire lot of assets in conjunction with pollutants, chemical materials in non-public care products, or even the food we devour. When pollutants enter the body, they may be capable of disrupt the endocrine tool, this is accountable for regulating hormones.

The endocrine tool is made from glands that produce hormones, that are chemical messengers that inform the body what to do. When pollutants disrupt the endocrine machine, they may be able to purpose the frame to produce an excessive amount of or too little of advantageous hormones, predominant to hormonal imbalances.

For instance, publicity to pollution like bisphenol-A (BPA) located in plastic boxes and canned food, can disrupt the producing of estrogen in ladies, leading to hormone-associated health problems like breast most cancers, endometriosis, and PCOS. Similarly, publicity to pesticides can disrupt the production of testosterone in men, number one to low libido, erectile dysfunction, and infertility.

Toxins can also purpose insulin resistance, that can result in weight gain and sort 2 diabetes. When the frame is exposed to immoderate ranges of pollutants, it may motive in ammation in the body, main to persistent fitness issues like autoimmune ailments, bronchial allergic reactions, and allergic reactions.

The correct records is that by way of decreasing your exposure to pollutants and helping your frame's natural detoxi cation strategies, you can decorate your hormonal balance. This may be executed through a combination of dietary and manner of existence modifications, as well as targeted nutritional nutritional dietary supplements and treatment alternatives.

Detoxi cation in naturopathy o ers a holistic technique to detoxifying the body and restoring hormonal stability. By figuring out and putting off pollution from the frame, assisting liver fitness, and selling healthy digestion, detoxi cation can help enhance strength stages, highbrow clarity, and wellknown health.

In surrender, the link among pollution and hormonal imbalances is a complicated one. However, via data how pollution can disrupt the endocrine system and enforcing detoxi cation techniques, you could assist your body's natural recovery procedures and gain pinnacle-high-quality health and well-being.

Foods and dietary supplements that promote hormonal stability

Hormonal imbalances can wreak havoc on your frame and mind, causing a number of signs and symptoms and signs and symptoms from fatigue and weight gain to temper swings and anxiety. Fortunately, there are numerous natural remedies that allow you to restore hormonal stability and beautify your average fitness and properly-being. Here are a number of the fine meals and nutritional dietary supplements to keep in thoughts incorporating into your diet:

1. Maca root: This Peruvian superfood is rich in nutrients, minerals, and vital fatty acids which can assist modify hormones, enhance energy levels, and improve temper. It's additionally a natural aphrodisiac and can improve sexual function in each women and men.

2. Flaxseeds: These tiny seeds are a super supply of ber, omega-3 fatty acids, and lignans, which might be compounds which can help balance estrogen tiers in the body.

They also have anti-in ammatory homes and might enhance heart fitness.

3. Cruciferous vegetables: Broccoli, cauli ower, Brussels sprouts, and awesome cruciferous greens are rich in indole-3-carbinol, a compound that could assist detoxify excess estrogen from the frame and decrease the danger of most cancers.

4. Ashwagandha: This adaptogenic herb has been used for hundreds of years in Ayurvedic remedy to assist stability hormones, reduce strain, and decorate immune function. It's additionally been demonstrated to decorate fertility in both women and men.

five. Omega-3 fatty acids: Found in fatty sh like salmon and sardines, similarly to in axseeds and chia seeds, the ones healthful fat can help lessen in ammation and

enhance mind feature. They've furthermore been confirmed to enhance hormonal stability

and fertility in girls.

6. Vitamin D: This vital nutrient is essential for keeping healthful hormone stages, especially in girls. It's moreover essential for bone health, immune function, and highbrow fitness.

7. Magnesium: This mineral is worried in over three hundred biochemical reactions in the body, at the side of hormone synthesis and law. It's additionally essential for muscle and nerve characteristic, bone health, and power manufacturing.

By incorporating those food and nutritional dietary supplements into your weight loss program, you may help repair hormonal stability and enhance your regular fitness and well-being. However, it is important to take into account that definitely all people's frame is di erent, and what works for one character may not paintings for a few different. It's always notable to artwork with a quali ed naturopathic medical doctor or holistic healthcare practitioner to create a customized plan that meets your specific goals and desires.

Lifestyle adjustments for hormonal stability

Our hormones play a important function in maintaining the general fitness and well-being of our frame. They control our temper, strength levels, weight, or maybe our pores and pores and skin health. Hormonal imbalances are a not unusual problem that a ects tens of millions of human beings global, primary to a number of fitness issues, together with weight advantage, acne, hair loss, and fatigue. However, making a few easy manner of lifestyles changes will let you stability your hormones obviously and decorate your trendy fitness.

The rst step closer to hormonal stability is to dispose of poisonous substances out of your eating regimen and way of life. You have to keep away from processed food, sugar, ca eine, alcohol, and distinct volatile materials that disrupt your hormones. Instead, cognizance on consuming a healthful food regimen wealthy in complete grains, surrender end result, greens, and lean protein. This will help to do away with pollutants from your body and assist hormonal stability.

Regular exercise is a few specific critical aspect of maintaining hormonal stability. Exercise allows to decorate blood waft, reduce strain, and enhance metabolism, all of which is probably vital for hormonal stability. You can choose any shape of exercise that you experience, which incorporates yoga, Pilates, weight training, or aerobic physical sports activities. Stress is a signi cant contributor to hormonal imbalances. Chronic strain can result in extended ranges of cortisol, a pressure hormone which can disrupt your hormones and motive weight benefit, pimples, and fatigue. Therefore, it's far important to control stress stages via using working in the direction of rest strategies at the side of meditation, deep respiration, or mindfulness.

Getting enough sleep is likewise critical for hormonal balance. Sleep deprivation can disrupt your hormones and cause a variety of health issues. Therefore, it is critical to get at the least 7-eight hours of uninterrupted sleep each night time.

In addition to the ones manner of lifestyles adjustments, positive herbal nutritional supplements and herbs can also assist to stability your hormones. Some of the maximum e ective dietary supplements for hormonal stability encompass omega-3 fatty acids, magnesium, zinc, and vitamins D. Herbs which encompass ashwagandha, maca root, and holy basil can also assist to stability your hormones simply.

In end, hormonal balance is important for retaining common fitness and health. By making some clean lifestyle adjustments, you could balance your hormones clearly and decorate your health. Remember to consume a healthful food plan, exercising regularly, control pressure, get enough sleep, and supplement with herbal herbs and nutritional dietary supplements.

Detoxification for Mental Clarity and Focus in Naturopathy

The link amongst pollution and thoughts characteristic

The hyperlink among pollutants and mind characteristic is a essential factor of detoxi cation in naturopathy. The mind is one of the most complex and crucial organs in the frame, liable for a extensive type of skills, from cognition and reminiscence to emotional law and behavior. However, pollution can intervene with the ones capabilities and reason pretty a number of neurological troubles, together with Parkinson's ailment, Alzheimer's sickness, and multiple sclerosis.

Toxins can enter the body through numerous property, collectively with the food we eat, the air we breathe, and the goods we use. They can gather in di erent organs and tissues, collectively with the thoughts, and disrupt their ordinary skills. For example, heavy metals like lead and mercury can damage the neurons and impair cognitive function, at the equal time as insecticides and herbicides can intervene with neurotransmitters and cause mood troubles.

Detoxi cation in naturopathy targets to dispose of those pollution from the body and repair the herbal balance of its structures. The liver and kidneys are the primary organs chargeable for detoxi cation, but other organs much like the pores and pores and skin, lungs, and lymphatic tool moreover play a vital characteristic. Naturopathic strategies to detoxi cation encompass dietary changes, herbal treatments, bodily treatment plans, and way of life modi cations.

A wholesome diet is essential for detoxi cation, because it gives the critical nutrients and antioxidants to assist the body's herbal detoxi cation tactics. Foods which can be wealthy in ber, nutrients, and minerals, together with give up stop result, vegetables, entire grains, and legumes, can help eliminate pollution from the body and decrease in ammation. On the opportunity hand, processed foods, re ned sugars, and trans fats can increase the burden on the liver and make contributions to the accumulation of pollution.

Herbal treatments can also useful resource in detoxi cation through supporting the liver and kidneys' talents and selling the removal of pollution. Milk thistle, dandelion root, and burdock root are a number of the herbs commonly applied in naturopathic medication for liver detoxi cation. Other herbs, along with ginger, turmeric, and garlic, have antiin ammatory and antioxidant homes that would guard the mind from damage due to pollutants.

Physical remedies, along with massage, acupuncture, and hydrotherapy, can also enhance the frame's detoxi cation techniques through improving circulate, lymphatic drainage, and sweating. These remedies can also lessen stress, it actually is a signi cant contributor to the buildup of pollution within the frame.

In summary, detoxi cation in naturopathy is a whole technique for natural restoration that considers the hyperlink among pollution and mind feature. By eliminating pollution from the body and restoring its natural stability, it can improve mind feature, mood, and common health. Whether you are looking for detoxi cation for weight loss, liver fitness, pores and pores and skin health, power and electricity, hormonal balance, intellectual readability and attention, breathing fitness, immune machine help, digestive health, or dependancy recuperation, naturopathic treatment can offer secure and e ective solutions.

Foods and supplements that promote highbrow readability and reputation

Foods and nutritional nutritional dietary supplements that promote intellectual clarity and recognition are critical for people in search of natural recuperation. The mind is the maximum essential organ in the frame, and its right functioning is crucial for common health and nicely being. To promote intellectual clarity and attention, we recommend incorporating speci c components and dietary supplements into your diet regime.

Firstly, you have to recognition on eating meals which might be rich in omega-3 fatty acids. These essential fat are important for thoughts health and can enhance cognitive function and memory retention. You can nd omega-3s in fatty sh like salmon, tuna, and mackerel, similarly to in nuts and seeds like chia seeds and axseed. Additionally, incorporating leafy vegetables like spinach, kale, and collard vegetables into your healthy eating plan can offer your body with vital vitamins like folate and diet K, which is probably regarded to sell cognitive characteristic.

Another crucial complement for intellectual clarity and cognizance is ca eine. Ca eine is a herbal stimulant that can decorate alertness and attention. You can nd ca eine in tea and co ee, or you can take it as a complement. However, it's far vital to take a look at that immoderate ca eine consumption can motive tension and restlessness, so it's miles important to consume it cautiously.

Additionally, adaptogenic herbs like ashwagandha, rhodiola rosea, and ginseng can help reduce stress, that's critical for retaining intellectual clarity and focus. Adaptogenic herbs artwork with the aid of way of regulating the frame's pressure reaction and might help enhance cognitive feature and reminiscence retention.

Lastly, incorporating antioxidant-rich food into your eating regimen can sell intellectual clarity and awareness. Antioxidants are vital for defensive the thoughts from oxidative pressure, that could harm thoughts cells and result in cognitive decline. Foods like berries, dark chocolate, and inexperienced tea are superb property of antioxidants and can assist decorate cognitive characteristic.

In give up, incorporating components and supplements that sell mental readability and recognition into your diet plan is important for natural restoration. Consuming meals rich in omega-3s, leafy greens, and antioxidants, further to taking dietary dietary supplements like ca eine and adaptogenic herbs, can help decorate cognitive feature, reminiscence retention, and reduce stress. By making the ones dietary changes, you may obtain pinnacle-rated thoughts fitness and commonplace fitness.

Chapter 5: Mindfulness And Cleansing

In present day day fast-paced international, it is easy to get caught up inside the hustle and bustle of regular life. We often neglect our health and nicely-being, most important to an accumulation of pollution in our our bodies. This can bring about some of health troubles, which embody weight advantage, liver troubles, pores and pores and pores and skin troubles, hormonal imbalances, intellectual fog, and respiration issues. Fortunately, there can be a natural approach to detoxify our our our bodies and beautify our commonplace fitness: mindfulness.

Mindfulness is the exercising of being fully gift in the moment, without judgment. It involves listening to your mind, emotions, and bodily sensations with a enjoy of interest and openness. By training mindfulness, we come to be more aware about our our our bodies and our environment, permitting us to make better options for our health.

One of the number one bene ts of mindfulness is stress reduce price. When we are careworn, our our bodies launch cortisol, a hormone which can have unfavourable e ects on our fitness. By operating closer to mindfulness, we are able to reduce our pressure stages, that would help to lower our cortisol stages and beautify our general fitness.

Another bene t of mindfulness is advanced digestion. When we are forced, our our our bodies divert blood ow far from our digestive tool, that would cause digestive issues. By training mindfulness, we are able to lessen our pressure ranges and enhance our digestion, important to higher nutrient absorption and regular fitness.

Mindfulness also can assist to beautify our intellectual clarity and interest. By being attentive to our mind and emotions, we can become greater privy to our intellectual united states and make better choices. This can bring about superior productiveness, higher relationships, and desired happiness.

In surrender, mindfulness is an critical tool for detoxi cation in naturopathy. By working towards mindfulness, we are able to reduce our pressure degrees, beautify our digestion, and improve our intellectual readability and recognition. Whether you're searching out to beautify your weight, liver fitness, pores and pores and skin health, electricity, hormonal stability, mental readability, breathing fitness, immune system assist, digestive fitness, or dependancy recovery, mindfulness let you acquire your goals. So why no longer provide it a try in recent times? Your body will thanks for it.

Detoxification for Respiratory Health in Naturopathy

How pollution have an effect at the breathing device

The respiration tool plays a essential characteristic in maintaining the body healthy and functioning nicely. It helps within the trade of oxygen and carbon dioxide, this is crucial for the body's survival. However, publicity to pollutants may also want to have a damaging e ect at the breathing device, vital to numerous fitness troubles.

Toxins are harmful substances that can be located within the air we breathe, food we consume, and merchandise we use. These pollutants can a ect the breathing gadget in numerous strategies. The maximum not unusual way toxins a ect the respiration device is through inhalation. When we breathe in pollution, they're capable of worsen and harm the lungs, main to breathing issues.

One of the maximum risky pollution for the respiration tool is cigarette smoke. Cigarette smoke includes hundreds of volatile chemical compounds, lots of that might bring about lung most cancers, persistent obstructive pulmonary infection (COPD), and different breathing troubles. Secondhand smoke additionally may be harmful, in particular for youngsters and those with breathing troubles.

Another toxin which can a ect the breathing tool is air pollution. Air pollutants can motive respiration issues together with hypersensitive reactions, bronchitis, and COPD. It can also increase the danger of lung maximum cancers.

Mold is each one-of-a-kind toxin that may a ect the respiration machine. Mold spores may be inhaled and reason breathing troubles collectively with allergies, allergic reactions, and fantastic lung infections.

Toxins also can a ect the immune system, making it di cult for the frame to ght o infections and diseases. This can reason respiratory infections which includes pneumonia and bronchitis.

To reduce the damaging e ects of pollution on the respiratory device, it's far vital to exercise detoxi cation. Detoxi cation can assist get rid of pollutants from the body and guide the immune device. Eating a healthful eating regimen, workout often, and retaining off smoking and exposure to pollution can also assist preserve the breathing machine healthy.

In end, pollution may additionally have a harmful e ect at the respiration tool, fundamental to numerous fitness troubles. To reduce the effect of pollutants at the respiratory device, it's miles crucial to exercising detoxi cation and take steps to guard the breathing gadget from pollution. By doing so, people can help their respiratory health and average well-being.

Foods and dietary supplements that promote respiration fitness

Respiratory fitness is essential for common properly-being. The breathing device incorporates the lungs, bronchi, trachea, and larynx, and it performs a crucial function in respiration and oxygen trade. The significance of retaining respiratory fitness cannot be overstated. In this subchapter, we are able to discover food and nutritional dietary supplements that might help promote breathing fitness.

1. Ginger

Ginger is a powerful anti-in ammatory agent that may assist reduce in ammation inside the respiration tract. It is also an e ective expectorant, because of this that it can assist loosen mucus and phlegm from the lungs, making it less complicated to breathe. Ginger can be ate up in severa paperwork, such as ginger tea, ginger ale, or ginger dietary supplements.

2. Turmeric

Turmeric is every one of a kind effective anti-in ammatory agent that could assist lessen in ammation inside the breathing tract. It consists of a compound called curcumin, which has been tested to have bene cial e ects on respiratory fitness. Turmeric can be fed on in various paperwork, together with turmeric tea, turmeric milk, or turmeric nutritional supplements.

three. Garlic

Garlic is each one-of-a-kind strong anti-in ammatory agent that can help lessen in ammation within the respiratory tract. It includes a compound known as allicin, which has been confirmed to have bene cial e ects on respiration health. Garlic may be ate up in numerous paperwork, together with uncooked garlic, garlic dietary nutritional dietary supplements, or garlic-infused food.

4. Vitamin C

Vitamin C is a effective antioxidant that could help guard the breathing machine from oxidative harm. It also can assist beautify the immune device, it really is important for respiration health. Vitamin C can be fed on in numerous paperwork, which include citrus give up result, kiwis, strawberries, or healthy dietweight-reduction plan C nutritional supplements.

five. Omega-three Fatty Acids

Omega-three fatty acids are vital for respiratory fitness because they help lessen in ammation within the respiration tract. They also can help beautify lung characteristic and reduce the hazard of breathing infections. Omega-three fatty acids can be consumed in various office work, at the side of fatty sh, axseeds, chia seeds, or omega-three dietary supplements.

In give up, keeping breathing fitness is crucial for commonplace nicely-being. Consuming ingredients and dietary supplements that sell respiration health can assist reduce in ammation, improve lung function, and lift the immune device. Incorporating those elements and nutritional supplements into your weight loss plan can help you maintain pinnacle-great breathing fitness.

Natural treatments for commonplace respiration conditions

If you're seeking out natural remedies to alleviate respiratory conditions, you've got were given come to the proper vicinity. In this subchapter, we are able to find out some of the maximum e ective natural remedies for common respiration conditions. These treatments were used for masses of years and characteristic installed to be pretty e ective in treating severa respiration ailments.

One of the most common respiratory conditions is bronchial allergies. Asthma is a persistent situation that a ects thousands and plenty of humans global. It is characterized with the resource of in ammation and narrowing of the airways, that could bring about wheezing, coughing, and di culty respiration. One of the first rate natural remedies for bronchial bronchial asthma is ginger. Ginger has anti-in ammatory homes which can assist lessen in ammation in the airways and decorate breathing. You can consume ginger in numerous office work, which include ginger tea, ginger tablets, or add it on your meals.

Another not unusual respiration scenario is bronchitis. Bronchitis is an in ammation of the bronchial tubes, which convey air to the lungs. It is commonly as a result of a viral or bacterial infection and might motive coughing, wheezing, and shortness of breath. One of the first rate herbal treatments for bronchitis is honey. Honey has antibacterial houses that would assist ght the infection and soothe the throat. You can add honey for your tea or devour it at once.

Sinusitis is another respiratory condition that a ects many humans. Sinusitis is an in ammation of the sinuses, which can be hole cavities in the skull. It can cause headaches, facial pain, and nasal congestion. One of the fantastic herbal remedies for sinusitis is eucalyptus oil. Eucalyptus oil has anti-in ammatory and decongestant homes that would help relieve nasal congestion and reduce in ammation. You can add a few drops of eucalyptus oil to heat water and inhale the steam.

In prevent, natural remedies may be especially e ective in treating numerous respiratory situations. Ginger, honey, and eucalyptus oil are only some of the various natural remedies that might help alleviate breathing ailments. However, it is crucial to consult your naturopathic medical doctor before attempting any natural remedies to make certain that they're constant for you.

Detoxification for Immune System Support in Naturopathy

The hyperlink among pollutants and immune device function

The link amongst pollutants and immune gadget characteristic is a critical aspect of herbal healing that desires to be explored. Toxins, whether or not or now not they'll be from the surroundings, food, or personal care merchandise, can signi cantly effect the immune machine's functioning, vital to diverse fitness troubles.

Our immune machine is liable for shielding us from dangerous bacteria, viruses, and special pathogens which can purpose diseases. However, at the identical time because the immune gadget is overloaded with pollution, its capability to ght o infections and illnesses is compromised, major to a weakened immune device.

Toxins can right now a ect the immune system through using negative the cells and tissues that make up the immune device. They can also disrupt the conversation a number of the di erent immune cells, main to miscommunication and confusion. This can bring about the immune machine attacking the frame's healthful cells and tissues, main to autoimmune diseases.

Additionally, pollution can purpose persistent in ammation in the body, which could further weaken the immune tool. Chronic in ammation can also cause severa health troubles consisting of coronary heart ailment, diabetes, and most cancers.

Detoxi cation in naturopathy is a entire method to addressing the hyperlink amongst pollutants and immune device characteristic. By removing pollutants from the frame thru numerous natural techniques including food regimen, exercising, and natural treatments, the immune gadget can feature optimally.

Detoxi cation also can help reduce in ammation inside the body, foremost to advanced immune device feature. It can also help liver characteristic, that is accountable tor

ltering pollutants from the frame.

In give up, the link among pollution and immune system characteristic can't be left out with reference to natural healing. Detoxi cation in naturopathy is a powerful tool that could assist cast off pollution from the body, major to advanced immune system function and common health. Whether you are trying to shed kilos, enhance liver or pores and pores and skin health, raise energy and strength, stability hormones, decorate mental clarity and attention, beneficial aid respiration or digestive fitness, or overcome dependancy, detoxi cation in naturopathy will will permit you to gain your health goals virtually.

Foods and dietary dietary supplements that promote immune device beneficial useful resource

Foods and nutritional dietary supplements that sell immune device beneficial useful resource are vital for the frame to ght toward pathogens and ailments obviously. These food and dietary dietary supplements may be included in a detoxi cation food plan to enhance the immune tool's characteristic and assist the frame put off pollutants e ectively.

One of the incredible elements for immune gadget help is garlic. It consists of allicin, a compound that has antiviral and antibacterial homes. Garlic additionally lets in to lessen in ammation within the body, that is crucial for immune tool fitness.

Another meals that promotes immune gadget guide is ginger. Ginger includes gingerol, which has antioxidant and anti-in ammatory homes that assist to reduce in ammation inside the frame and growth the immune tool's feature. Ginger additionally allows decorating digestion, this is vital for eliminating pollutants from the frame.

Vitamin C is a important nutrient for immune gadget health, and it may be located in lots of materials, collectively with citrus give up result, kiwi, papaya, and strawberries. Vitamin C permits to beautify the manufacturing of white blood cells, which can be important for ghting o infections.

Probiotics also are essential for immune tool fitness, as they help to sell the growth of healthy micro organism within the intestine. Fermented meals which include sauerkraut, kimchi, and ke r are brilliant belongings of probiotics.

Supplements also may be used to sell immune gadget guide. Vitamin D is important for immune device fitness, and masses of human beings are de cient on this nutrient. Taking a eating regimen D supplement can help to enhance the immune system's feature.

Zinc is a few different essential nutrients for immune tool fitness, and it is able to be observed in food collectively with oysters, red meat, and pumpkin seeds. Taking a zinc supplement also can help to beautify the immune device's characteristic.

In precis, meals and dietary supplements that promote immune device help are crucial for herbal restoration and detoxi cation. Including those components and nutritional supplements in a detoxi cation weight loss plan can assist to beautify the immune system's function and promote standard fitness and nicely-being.

Chapter 6: Lifestyle Adjustments For Immune Tool Help

The immune device is your body's protection mechanism in opposition to risky pathogens, viruses, and bacteria. When your immune device is inclined, you're extra vulnerable to infections and illnesses. Therefore, it is critical to attend to your immune machine to make certain it's miles functioning optimally. In this bankruptcy, we're able to communicate diverse way of life modifications that you can make to help your immune machine absolutely.

1. Maintain a Healthy Diet

Your diet plays a critical characteristic in assisting your immune device. A healthful eating regimen need to include entire components together with give up result, vegetables, entire grains, lean proteins, and wholesome fat. These food are wealthy in vital vitamins and minerals that help to reinforce your immune device. Vitamin C, weight-reduction plan D, and zinc are specially vital for immune function. You can reap those nutrients from meals such as citrus quit result, leafy veggies, nuts, seeds, and oily sh.

2. Get Enough Sleep

Sleep is crucial for a healthy immune system. When you sleep, your body protection and regenerates its cells, together with immune cells. Lack of sleep can weaken your immune device, developing your susceptibility to infections and illnesses. Aim to get 7-eight hours of sleep every night time to resource your immune fitness.

three. Exercise Regularly

Regular exercising has numerous fitness bene ts, together with boosting your immune tool. Exercise permits to growth blood ow and float, which lets in to move immune cells during the body. Exercise additionally allows to reduce stress, which could have a bad effect on your immune machine. Aim to get as a minimum 30 minutes of mild workout each day to help your immune health.

4. Reduce Stress

Chronic strain may additionally moreover have a horrible effect to your immune gadget. Stress triggers the release of cortisol, a hormone that suppresses the immune tool. Therefore, it's miles important to nd approaches to manipulate your strain tiers. Meditation, yoga, deep breathing sporting activities, and spending time in nature are all e ective strategies to lessen pressure and help your immune device.

5. Avoid Smoking and Alcohol

Smoking and alcohol can weaken your immune device, making you greater prone to infections and illnesses. Smoking damages the lungs, making it more difficult for the body to ght o breathing infections. Alcohol can also suppress the immune tool, making it extra difficult for the body to ght o infections. Therefore, it is critical to keep away from smoking and restrict your alcohol intake to assist your immune fitness.

In give up, making manner of life adjustments which include retaining a healthy weight-reduction plan, getting enough sleep, workout regularly, lowering stress, and heading off smoking and alcohol can all help to assist your immune tool truly. By searching after your immune system, you may beautify your chosen fitness and properly-being.

Detoxification for Digestive Health in Naturopathy

The feature of the digestive gadget in detoxification

The digestive machine performs a signi cant function in detoxi cation. It is responsible for breaking down meals into nutrients and eliminating waste merchandise. However, it additionally has the crucial mission of identifying risky substances and eliminating them from the body.

The liver is the precept detoxifying organ inside the body, and the digestive device performs a vital position in assisting its function. The liver produces bile, that is saved within the gallbladder and launched into the small gut to useful useful aid in the digestion of fat. Bile additionally enables to dispose of toxins and waste merchandise from the body.

The small gut is wherein maximum of the vitamins from food are absorbed into the bloodstream. However, it's also a net site wherein pollution may be absorbed. If the digestive gadget isn't functioning optimally, pollutants can growth in the body and reason quite some of fitness troubles.

The big intestine, or colon, is liable for putting off waste merchandise from the body. A healthful colon is critical for correct detoxi cation. If waste merchandise aren't eliminated e ciently, they might building up and purpose in ammation and precise fitness problems.

The digestive gadget is based on a wholesome balance of gut bacteria to characteristic optimally. These bacteria assist to break down meals and eliminate waste products. They also play a important function in helping the immune device and stopping the boom of volatile bacteria and viruses.

To useful resource the digestive tool's function in detoxi cation, it's miles critical to devour a wholesome food plan this is rich in ber, nutrients, and antioxidants. Foods which are excessive in processed sugars, re ned carbohydrates, and saturated fat can disrupt the steadiness of gut bacteria and impair the digestive device's feature.

In addition to a wholesome weight-reduction plan, ordinary exercising, stress manage, and getting sufficient sleep are essential for assisting the digestive tool's function in detoxi cation. These way of life factors can help to reduce in ammation, guide intestine health, and promote pinnacle-rated liver function.

In cease, the digestive device plays a critical function in detoxi cation and customary fitness. By assisting the digestive system thru wholesome consuming, way of life conduct, and natural treatments, we're capable of decorate its characteristic and promote very last detoxi cation.

Foods and dietary dietary supplements that sell digestive fitness

Foods and dietary supplements that sell digestive health are crucial for folks which are attempting to find natural recuperation. A wholesome digestive device is essential for ordinary properly-being and may help prevent an entire lot of health issues consisting of constipation, bloating, and indigestion.

One of the nice meals for promoting digestive health is ber-rich give up result and greens. These components provide the frame with the critical ber to maintain the digestive tract moving without problems. Foods which encompass apples, pears, bananas, broccoli, and Brussels sprouts are all tremendous sources of ber.

Probiotics are each different critical supplement for digestive fitness. Probiotics are bene cial bacteria that stay inside the intestine and help keep the digestive gadget functioning well. They may be determined in fermented components which include yogurt, ke r, and sauerkraut. If you do now not consume sufficient probiotics thru your diet plan, you may also take a probiotic complement.

Digestive enzymes are some other important complement for promoting digestive fitness. These enzymes help harm down meals within the digestive tract, making it plenty less complicated for the body to soak up vitamins. Digestive enzyme dietary supplements are available in tablet form and can be eager about food to aid digestion.

In addition to these ingredients and nutritional dietary supplements, it's also crucial to stay hydrated. Drinking loads of water lets in preserve the digestive tract lubricated and transferring easily. It's endorsed to drink at the least 8 glasses of water an afternoon.

In quit, incorporating meals and dietary supplements that sell digestive health into your eating regimen can help prevent some of digestive issues and promote overall nicely-being. By consuming a food regimen rich in ber, consuming probiotics and digestive enzymes, ingesting bone broth, and staying hydrated, you may help maintain your digestive tool functioning properly.

Natural remedies for common digestive conditions

Digestive troubles are a common health hassle that a ects people of each age. Many people su er from digestive situations which encompass bloating, constipation, diarrhea, and gas. The accurate information is that there are herbal remedies which can assist alleviate the ones signs and signs.

1. Ginger: Ginger has anti-in ammatory and antimicrobial houses that may help soothe the digestive tool. It can help relieve nausea, vomiting, and bloating. You can upload ginger for your tea, smoothies, or soups.

2. Peppermint: Peppermint is every exclusive herbal treatment that would assist soothe the digestive device. It can help relieve bloating, gas, and indigestion. You can drink peppermint tea or upload peppermint oil to your water.

3. Fennel: Fennel is a herbal remedy that can help relieve bloating, gas, and constipation. It can assist stimulate digestion and decrease in ammation. You can upload fennel seeds for your tea or meals.

4. Probiotics: Probiotics are bene cial micro organism which could assist decorate gut fitness. They can help relieve digestive problems which encompass bloating, constipation, and diarrhea. You can take probiotic nutritional supplements or eat

fermented food collectively with yogurt, kimchi, and sauerkraut.

five. Aloe Vera: Aloe vera has anti-in ammatory homes that can assist soothe the digestive machine. It can assist relieve constipation, diarrhea, and acid re ux. You can drink aloe vera juice or add aloe vera gel in your smoothies.

6. Chamomile: Chamomile is any other herbal remedy that might help relieve digestive problems. It can assist reduce in ammation, relieve bloating, and soothe the intestine. You can drink chamomile tea or add chamomile oil on your water.

In give up, herbal remedies can be e ective in treating digestive problems. However, it's far vital to are seeking advice from a quali ed naturopath earlier than trying any herbal treatments. They can guide you at the right dosage and make sure that the treatments might not have interaction with any drugs you're taking. Remember, herbal remedies are a complementary treatment and want to now not update medical remedy.

Chapter 7: Addiction Recovery In Naturopathy

The hyperlink among pollution and dependancy

The hyperlink amongst pollutants and addiction is a complicated, but often not noted, detail of natural recuperation. Our our our our bodies are designed to eliminate pollution thru severa organs together with the liver, kidneys, and pores and pores and skin. However, even as we're exposed to an excessive amount of pollutants, our our our bodies can end up crushed, main to a construct-up of pollutants in our device. This assemble-up can result in severa health problems, along with addiction.

Toxins can a ect the mind in many methods, essential to dependancy. For instance, alcohol and pills can harm the thoughts's reward device, main to an dependancy cycle. Similarly, environmental pollutants such as heavy metals and insecticides can a ect the thoughts's neurotransmitters, most critical to a complicated hazard of addiction. In addition, pollution can weaken the immune device, making it greater di cult for the body to ght o dependancy.

Detoxi cation is an critical part of addiction recovery in naturopathy. Detoxi cation involves the removal of pollution from the body, permitting the frame to heal and restore itself to most suitable fitness. Detoxi cation may be finished through numerous strategies, which includes eating regimen, exercise, and nutritional supplements.

One of the maximum e ective strategies to detoxify the frame is thru a healthy eating regimen. A weight loss plan wealthy in cease give up end result, vegetables, and complete grains can provide the frame with vital vitamins even as moreover helping to put off toxins. Similarly, regular exercising can assist to stimulate the frame's natural detoxi cation strategies, assisting to remove pollutants from the body.

Supplements also can be an e ective way to support detoxi cation. Supplements which encompass milk thistle and dandelion root can help to guide liver feature, even as probiotics can help to repair the stableness of healthy micro organism inside the gut, supporting to help digestive fitness.

In quit, the link among pollutants and addiction is an vital problem of herbal restoration. Detoxi cation is an essential part of dependancy recuperation, and it is able to be finished thru diverse strategies, which incorporates healthy eating plan, exercise, and supplements. By eliminating pollutants from the body, we are capable of help our body's natural restoration procedures, predominant to progressed fitness and nicely-being.

Foods and supplements that resource in dependancy recuperation

Addiction is a excessive fitness situation that a ects tens of millions of people global. Whether it is alcohol, capsules, or some different addictive substance, the device of recovery may be tough. While there may be no unmarried treatment for addiction, there are fine food and dietary supplements that may resource in the recuperation manner.

The rst key nutrient to keep in mind is omega-3 fatty acids. These vital fats are placed in fatty sh, nuts, and seeds. Studies have proven that omega-3s can assist reduce in ammation inside the thoughts, that may aid in addiction recuperation. They can also assist enhance mood and reduce anxiety and despair, which are not unusual symptoms and signs and signs and symptoms of withdrawal.

Another vital nutrient is amino acids. These constructing blocks of protein are essential for the producing of neurotransmitters inside the mind, which play a role in dependancy and recuperation. Speci cally, the amino acid tyrosine can help decorate mood and energy stages, on the identical time as tryptophan can help lessen cravings and enhance sleep. Foods rich in the ones amino acids embody meat, sh, eggs, and legumes. In addition to those key vitamins, there are numerous nutritional dietary supplements that can beneficial useful resource in addiction recovery. One of the maximum well-known is N-acetylcysteine (NAC), that is a shape of the amino acid cysteine. NAC has been demonstrated to reduce cravings and enhance temper in human beings with addiction. It additionally has antioxidant houses, which could help shield the mind from damage due to drug and alcohol use.

Another complement to recollect is magnesium. This critical mineral is concerned in over 3 hundred biochemical reactions in the frame, which embody the ones associated with temper and sleep. Studies have verified that magnesium can assist lessen anxiety and enhance sleep exquisite, every of which may be essential for addiction recovery.

Finally, probiotics are some other essential complement to go through in thoughts. These bene cial micro organism can assist enhance gut health, this is vital for essential health and properly being. Studies have additionally set up that probiotics can assist reduce cravings and enhance temper in individuals with dependancy.

In stop, while there is no single cure for dependancy, there are top notch meals and nutritional nutritional dietary supplements that might useful aid within the recovery gadget. By incorporating those key nutrients into your healthy dietweight-reduction plan and taking the proper dietary dietary dietary supplements, you can aid your body's herbal healing techniques and beautify your possibilities of a a hit healing.

Chapter 8: The Forgotten Ancestral Medicine

Have you ever at a loss for words how our ancestors, without get entry to to trendy medical era, had been able to live healthy and cope with numerous illnesses? Well, they grew to become to the most historical and natural medicine: naturopathy. Now, what exactly is naturopathy and why is it so applicable in recent times?

Naturopathy is a department of medicine that makes a speciality of the body's innate capability to heal itself. Rather than definitely treating the symptoms and signs of an infection, it seeks to deal with the inspiration cause of health problems, encouraging a holistic and proactive technique to properly-being. In essence, it is a medicinal drug that promotes concord among frame, thoughts and spirit.

You may be wondering, why, if it is so powerful and natural, has naturopathy been forgotten for good-bye? Well, within the hustle and bustle of current life and with the emergence of allopathic treatment, we were delivered about trust that the answer to our fitness issues lies in rapid-appearing drugs and advanced surgical strategies. However, as generation advances, we're starting to apprehend the energy of nature and historic traditions for fitness and nicely-being.

Think about it for a second, have you ever ever observed the way you revel in after a walk in the woods or after ingesting a plate of glowing, natural food? That feeling of revitalization and power isn't always any coincidence. Your frame is reacting to the recovery power of nature.

To recognize naturopathy is to recognize that our roots, our essence, is in element related to the herbal global. By ignoring this fact, we've got distanced ourselves from our very very very own fitness. The purpose of this bankruptcy, therefore, is to remind you of this effective tool at your disposal and that will help you find out how you could harness it to enhance your lifestyles.

But you do not want to take my phrase for it. Throughout the subsequent chapters, you can discover how naturopathy has been tested and validated by way of infinite research and empirical proof. Together, we're able to get to the lowest of the secrets and techniques and techniques and techniques of naturopathy and display how you could exercise them on your each day lifestyles. By the surrender, I assure you that you wlll be satisfied that the decision to move down the path of naturopathy is one of the wisest alternatives you may ever make.

Before I preserve, I would love to pause and ask you, are you equipped to open your mind to a one of a kind approach to health and properly being? If so, you are about to embark on a fascinating journey inside the route of knowledge your frame and the manner nature will let you acquire a more fit and extra pleasant lifestyles.

Remember, my pal, health is a adventure, not a vacation spot. So buckle up and get prepared for an exciting journey thru the superb essence of naturopathy.

It is crucial to emphasize that naturopathy isn't a present day introduction. As I cited, it has its roots within the clinical practices of historical cultures, which understood the importance of living in harmony with nature. Let's take a look at what some scholars within the statistics of medicine have to mention about this fascinating state of affairs.

In his e-book "History of Natural Medicine" (2010), historian James Whorton makes an extensive exploration of the way cultures collectively with Indian, Chinese and Greek applied naturopathic requirements in their fitness practices. According to Whorton, naturopathy is the compendium and refinement of this ancestral information.

Likewise, in "Naturopathy in Antiquity" (2015), herbal treatment professional Linda A. Johnson argues that a lot of cutting-edge-day naturopathic practices have direct parallels to historical Egyptian and Persian treatments. Surprising, is not it? It's no longer a newly determined direction, it's miles a forgotten path that we're remembering.

Maybe you sense a hint beaten proper now. It can be masses to soak up, but isn't it thrilling to recall how masses our ancestors knew approximately the human frame and herbal health?

So what modified, and why did we move from herbal treatment to remedy so counting on technology and chemical compounds? These are charming questions so you may be explored intensive in later chapters. For now, suffice it to mention that the economic revolution and clinical advances with the aid of some way took us a long way from the very essence of our health.

Returning to naturopathy, there may be a few component I would like to consciousness on. And this is that this problem, even though it appeals to nature and its techniques, isn't always at odds with technology. On the opposite, more and more studies help its effectiveness. In "The Role of Naturopathy in Modern Medicine" (2021), Dr. David Schleich highlights how current studies is validating what naturopathic practitioners have acknowledged for loads of years: that a holistic, nature-based totally approach may be pretty powerful in keeping and restoring fitness.

In addition, naturopathy is not approximately rejecting traditional medicine, but to supplement it, to are seeking a greater balanced and preventive technique. Of route, usually for the benefit of your nicely-being.

I wish this a long way you're even more intrigued and excited with the useful resource of all that naturopathy has to provide. I promise you will now not be disappointed. There remains lots extra to study, discover and find out. So, are you equipped to move forward in this journey?

Isn't it wonderful to suppose that every one that is indoors our attain?

Let me provide you with a greater tangible example to further make clear the essence of naturopathy and the way it is able to gain us. Imagine you have a small plant in your home, probably this sort of cute succulents which might be so well-known now. How would possibly you take care of it? Would you feed it chemicals and keep it out of the sunlight hours? Probably no longer. You realize that the plant wishes daylight, water, and nutrient-rich soil to thrive. You need to understand that its nicely-being depends on the stability of these elements.

What if I knowledgeable you that you are like that plant? You, too, need a wholesome, balanced surroundings to thrive. That is the essence of naturopathy: to offer you with the device to create that surroundings and help you thrive.

However, naturopathy does no longer claim to be a miracle treatment. Like the whole lot in existence, it requires time, staying power and commitment. In his ebook "The Truth About Naturopathy" (2018), Dr. Michael T. Murray reminds us that naturopathy is a exercising that calls for our energetic participation. It isn't always about taking a pill and looking for the whole lot to get better. It is set making aware adjustments in our lives and walking in the direction of a rustic of properly being.

You are in all likelihood asking yourself: how are we able to placed this into exercise? How can naturopathy be applied in day by day life? Very top questions, my costly reader, and I promise we can answer them. But first, it's miles vital that we recognize the inspiration of naturopathy.

Speaking of knowledge, an historical Chinese proverb includes thoughts that announces, "The realistic doctor does not remedy the illness, he remedies the future". Isn't that an exciting manner of looking at matters? What if, in desire to focusing actually on treating the symptoms, we sought to apprehend and cope with the underlying reasons of our ailments?

This is exactly the method that naturopathy proposes, and it's miles what we're able to discover inside the next chapter. But first, permit me leave you with a totally closing concept on our cutting-edge difficulty count number.

Naturopathy is an invite. An invitation to take price of your health, to apprehend that you are a holistic being and that each difficulty of your life influences your properly-being. And, like several invitation, you could acquire or reject it. But, do not you discovered it's far properly worth exploring it, on your nicely being and that of these you need?

I am here to accompany you on this adventure, that will help you smooth doubts, conquer boundaries and, in the end, find out a more wholesome and more harmonious way of dwelling. And continuously with a grin, because of the fact as you'll examine in a destiny bankruptcy, laughter is also a powerful form of medicine. Let's maintain going on this adventure, each step of the manner.

Perhaps this concept of looking at your fitness and health in this kind of holistic and natural manner may additionally moreover seem a bit overwhelming or maybe unexpected. You also can revel in like an explorer embarking on a journey right into a present day international. However, I need you to understand which you aren't by myself on this journey. I is probably right here with you, sharing the lights I even have accumulated by myself adventure, illuminating the route on the way to discover your very very own.

And not handiest that, my highly-priced reader. I need you to comprehend that you already have the statistics and equipment crucial to embark in this journey. As I stated in advance, naturopathy isn't about learning some problem without a doubt new or distant places. Rather, it is approximately remembering and rediscovering the ancient wisdoms that our species has amassed over hundreds of years, wisdoms that we might also additionally have forgotten in our modern-day-day, traumatic lives. Like the plant that desires sun, water and nutrients, you too intuitively recognize what you want to thrive.

You may be asking your self, "How can I do not forget those wisdoms? How can I learn how to concentrate to my frame and offer it with what it desires?" These are valuable questions, and I commend you for asking them. They are signs and signs and signs and symptoms that you are equipped to embark in this adventure, prepared to take an energetic role on your properly-being.

In the subsequent financial ruin, we are able to begin to find out those questions and in addition. We will dive into the terrific symphony that is our frame, to understand how every organ, each cell, performs a note in this harmonious melody we name lifestyles.

And when you start to understand the song, you will be one step within the course of becoming the conductor of the orchestra of your private properly-being.

I am excited to embark on this adventure with you. Together, we are able to discover, study and growth. And recall, that is a journey of pleasure and interest. So permit me ask you a question: Are you equipped for the following financial ruin, are you ready to find out the awesome symphony of the human frame and find out how you can assist your body play the maximum lovely melody?

If your answer is sure, then permit's wait now not. Gather your adventurous spirit, encompass your hobby, and allow me take you via the doorways of this new global. See you inside the next chapter, my buddy - see then you definately!

Chapter 9: The Symphony Of The Body

Now, steeply-priced buddy, I invite you to contemplate your frame no longer as a easy collection of components, however as a symphony in movement. Every be conscious your cells play, every rhythm your organs generate, is a part of a herbal artwork of art of endless complexity and marvel. Isn't that interesting? Doesn't it fill you with awe and gratitude for the incredible tool you are lucky sufficient to inhabit? And most importantly, does no longer it urge you to observe greater, to sharpen your knowledge and understand for your frame and to learn how to take higher care of it?

You may be thinking why it is crucial to recognize our organic tool within the context of naturopathy. Actually, the answer is simple: with a view to cope with our body in a manner this is in concord with its herbal functioning, we first want to understand the manner it works. Just as you can not behavior an orchestra with out information how the devices are executed and the manner they sound collectively, you can not efficaciously conduct your very personal health without information the premise of your biology.

The human body, within the beginning appearance, might also moreover seem rather complicated, with its lots and lots of cells, organs and structures going for walks together seamlessly. But what if I knowledgeable you that the entirety out of your fingertips to the nucleus of your cells follows a series of patterns and rhythms as harmonious and synchronized as a Beethoven symphony? In his 'The Body: A Guide for Occupants' (2019), Bill Bryson invitations us to contemplate the surprise of our very own bodies and apprehend their excellent complexity. And like Bryson, these days I want to ask you to embark on a journey of discovery and wonder, a journey in which you can learn how to 'pay attention' and 'apprehend' the symphony of your body.

Understanding our body, expensive reader, is not a easy project. It is a charming and difficult journey, entire of wonders and discoveries which can exchange the manner you stay and cope with yourself. But it's far a journey definitely nicely well worth taking. As Socrates stated, "The mystery of fitness for thoughts and frame isn't to regret the past, no longer to fear approximately the destiny, or not to assume problem, but to stay in the present moment accurately and extensively." And to stay as it need to be and considerably, we need to apprehend our body and the manner to hold it in stability.

Therefore, I urge you to open your thoughts and coronary coronary heart as we delve into the mysteries of our natural device. Pay interest, ask questions and, chiefly, have a laugh. Because gaining knowledge of approximately our body must now not be a humdrum and tedious task. On the other, it need to be a adventure entire of a laugh and surprise, a journey that evokes us to take better care of ourselves and live extra wholesome, happier lives.

So we're prepared, proper? Let's get to it! Although, in advance than I get into the data, permit me assist you to know one hassle. As the great Dr. Deepak Chopra said in "The Prescription for Life" (2001), "every mobile in your frame is eavesdropping for your thoughts." This concept is important, due to the fact what we expect, how we feel and the way we apprehend the area has a actual and tangible impact on our frame. Don't you find out it fascinating?

Our adventure begins on the most primary stage, that of the cells. Imagine for a 2d, if you can, that you are a large and which you have the capability to get closer and inside the direction of your body till you could see the person cells. What would no longer or no longer it's like? Can you agree with? What you will discover, steeply-priced reader, is a miniature universe. Each cellular in your frame is sort of a bustling city, with plenty of tactics occurring every 2nd. Cells are complete of tiny structures called organelles, every with a crucial function. Did you recognise, for instance, that during every of your cells there's a form of strength plant, referred to as a mitochondrion, that generates the power your body desires to function? It's absolutely fantastic!

Now, permit's pause right here. I ask you to close your eyes and believe all the cells to your body difficult at art work, generating strength, putting off waste, repairing themselves. Doesn't it make you revel in a feel of surprise and gratitude for your frame?

But what about the device that controls some of the ones functions? I am referring, of path, to the mind. That stunning organ this is on the back of every concept, each sensation, each choice we make. In his ebook "The Brain's Way of Healing" (2015), Dr. Norman Doidge indicates us how our thoughts is an organ of superb plasticity, capable of learning, adapting and restoration itself. And this, my buddy, is in which naturopathy and holistic medicinal drug come into play. By facts how our thoughts works and the way it communicates with the rest of our frame, we are able to discover strategies to sell its most dependable functioning and recovery capability.

Don't you find out it fascinating? All this can look like plenty to digest, but don't worry. Let's take it little by little, and collectively we are going to discover the secrets and techniques of our frame and the way to take the excellent possible care of it. So, take a breath, smile, and let's flow into on. Are you equipped?

Okay, let's circulate on, going a chunk deeper into this thrilling journey. Let me remind you that we're on this together, gaining knowledge of, coming across, developing. Are you playing the adventure as a lot as I am? I desire you are.

Now, if you idea cells and the mind had been the final frontier, permit me allow you to know about the tool that connects they all: the nervous system. This first rate wiring is like your frame's information dual carriageway. Everything that takes place on your body, from the feeling of heat to your fingers even as you maintain a warm cup of espresso, in your body's quick response at the same time as you turn away from a falling object, is all way to your nerve-racking device.

When exploring the sector of neuroscience, one can't assist however wonder. Think, for instance, of the synapse, the area wherein one neuron communicates with any other. As Eric Kandel factors out in his e-book "In Search of Memory" (2006), every of these tiny junctions is a worldwide unto itself, with complex molecular device that allows data to go together with the go with the flow from one cell to each different. Every belief you've got were given, every emotion you experience, is the quit stop result of hundreds of plenty of these synapses occurring right now. It's amazing, isn't always it?

Chapter 10: The Power Of Balance

Have you ever heard of Yin and Yang, my friend? Have you ever perceived their dance in the wind ruffling the leaves of the bushes or within the coming and going of the waves of the ocean? If your solution is "no", no problem! If it is "positive", you then really sincerely already realise a touch of its magic. Yin and Yang, important principles of Taoism, an historical Chinese philosophical and religious way of life, represent the two opposing and complementary forces that represent all factors and phenomena of existence.

In "The Tao of Physics" (1975), Fritjof Capra invitations us to recognize how Eastern ideas, together with Yin and Yang, discover a unexpected echo within the discoveries of contemporary-day quantum physics. But, we do no longer need to be physicists to recognize the relevance of Yin and Yang in our each day lives. I bet you have were given already skilled their interaction on your every day existence.

Imagine a mountain. Its pinnacle, exposed to the sun, would possibly represent Yang: slight, lively, masculine. The base, inside the color, is probably Yin: the darkish, the receptive, the lady. But may additionally the mountain in truth be a mountain with out its pinnacle or its base? Likewise, we couldn't exist with out the ordinary interplay of Yin and Yang in our lives.

Why is this critical? Well, spotting and facts the interaction of Yin and Yang in our lives may be the first step to carrying out a stability an notable way to without a doubt effect our nicely-being. And here is the vital issue: stability. In "The Wisdom of the Tao" (2006), Ming-Dao Deng reminds us that when Yin and Yang are balanced, they float in harmony and nourish existence. When one predominates over the opposite, imbalance results in chaos.

But how do we translate all this into our every day lives? I advocate a concept take a look at. Think of a normal day for your life, how does Yin and Yang take place? Is the strain of your method, the traffic, the frenetic activity, the example of Yang? Is the calm of your house, the sleep, the time of relaxation and rest, the manifestation of Yin? Now, do you experience that one predominates over the other?

If you understand an imbalance, do not worry. Herein lies the splendor of the Yin Yang philosophy. It is not static, it's miles a manual to waft and harmony, and extremely good of all, we have the functionality to move and regulate the quantities on our life board. Together, we're capable of find out how we're capable of observe Yin and Yang to regain balance and experience a fuller, extra colorful lifestyles. I assure this may be an adventure like no other.

Continuing our conversation, my friend, the philosophy of Yin and Yang isn't always genuinely the recognition of opposing forces. Isn't it charming? Both elements comprise the seed of the opportunity, which reminds us of the impermanence of the whole lot and the ordinary possibility of exchange.

Do you undergo in thoughts ever being so without a doubt satisfied that you felt like your heart might explode? That, my highly-priced reader, is a second of herbal Yang. But even in that immediate of natural delight, Yin is present, ready its flip to emerge, similar to the disappointment that sometimes follows moments of excessive happiness. And the same is real the alternative way round. In the darkest moments, there can be commonly the seed of moderate.

In "The Book of Tao" (4th century BCE), Lao-Tse teaches us to understand this go with the flow of Yin and Yang, to discover the route of least resistance, the Tao. Imagine yourself floating in a river. If you conflict inside the course of the current-day-day, you'll exhaust your self and might even sink. But, in case you allow your self go with the waft of the river, you will flow into with out problems and style.

Now, how can we use this information to decorate our lives? Let me take you via an afternoon on your lifestyles, with the eyes of Yin and Yang.

Have you ever woken up within the morning and felt simply exhausted, even after a entire night time time's sleep? There may be too much Yang on your life. Stress, constant interest and stimulation can drain your strength. In this situation, you need more Yin: relaxation, stillness, and self-care.

Conversely, if you feel listless, unmotivated and slow, there may be an excessive amount of Yin for your lifestyles. Here, you want more Yang: workout, highbrow stimulation, and socialization.

The poet William Blake in his artwork "The Marriage of Heaven and Hell" (1790-1793) recommended us that we need each heaven and hell to enjoy life in its fullness. Similarly, we need each Yin and Yang to stay a balanced and whole existence.

Of path, finding this stability is not an clean or sincere path. It calls for self-know-how, staying strength and, surely, kindness to yourself. But I promise you, that is a adventure actually really worth taking. Are you inclined to move earlier and find out how Yin and Yang can deliver balance and harmony to your existence?

Nutrition and Naturopathy: Conscious Eating for a Vibrant Life

Think about it for a second, how normally an afternoon do you devour? How often in keeping with week? And in a year? The numbers are lovely, are not they? Now, keep in mind that every of those times, each chew you are taking, is an opportunity to beautify your health, to vibrate with more energy, to boost your immune device, to stability your thoughts and feelings. Sounds attractive, does not it?

Now, how is it viable to acquire all this with our food regimen by myself? Therein lies the magic of conscious vitamins, a critical part of naturopathy. It isn't honestly a rely of filling the belly to put off starvation, however of expertise that every meals we consume has an impact on our organism, which can be useful or risky. Conscious eating is knowing that we're what we devour, absolutely.

If we take a look at our body to a vehicle, let's imagine that vitamins is the gasoline that keeps it on foot. Have you ever tried to location diesel in a fuel automobile? Probably no longer, due to the fact you understand that it might harm the engine. Similarly, we should be conscious that no longer all meals are appropriate for our frame.

Author and nutrients expert Michael Pollan, in his ebook "In Defense of Food" (2008), sums up this idea superbly: "Eat meals. Not an excessive amount of. Especially plants." This is the critical principle of conscious vitamins: consume actual meals, in its maximum natural united states of america possible, in moderate portions and with a predominance of flowers. Simple, right? Yet we frequently neglect the ones easy mind in our busy cutting-edge-day-day global. How many times have you ever eaten in a day without even expertise what you have been consuming, or with out listening to the manner you revel in after eating?

This is wherein naturopathy and vitamins come together. It's approximately reconnecting with our our our bodies, about expertise what we really want to nourish us, in desire to simply fill us up. As naturopaths, we agree with that nature gives us with the whole thing we want to live wholesome. Did you recognize that most modern day illnesses, from diabetes to coronary heart sickness, are without delay related to healthy dietweight-reduction plan?

I'm positive you're eager to investigate greater about this captivating difficulty remember. Are you organized to discover how you could remodel your lifestyles through conscious consuming? How can you switch every meal into an act of affection and deal with your self? Then permit's dive into this thrilling global of nutrition and naturopathy. It's time to nourish our body and soul in a manner that clearly honors the exceptional device this is our body.

Let me take you on a charming journey. Imagine we're in a tropical rainforest teeming with an superb sort of flowers. Each of these plant life has a very unique feature, and each contributes to the health and strength of the atmosphere as an entire. Some provide food for animals, others purify the air, and however others feature houses for severa species. This biodiversity is crucial to life.

Similarly, our our our bodies want a whole lot of nutrients to stay wholesome and colorful. Each nutrition, each mineral, every kind of protein or fiber has a completely unique characteristic in our our our bodies. As T. Colin Campbell in his ebook "The China Study" (2005), a nutrient-rich, plant-based totally totally weight-reduction plan can prevent or perhaps contrary maximum of the persistent diseases that plague current society.

If we skip once more to our wooded area metaphor, recollect now which you begin pulling up flora at random, without considering their function inside the environment. Soon, the wooded place would begin to die. The same takes region to our frame at the same time as we feed ourselves in an unbalanced and subconscious manner. Our inner "surroundings" becomes unbalanced, and this is even as illnesses seem.

I do no longer need you to be scared. On the opposite, I want you to enjoy the delight of facts that you have the power to keep your frame healthful and vibrant virtually through what you select out to vicinity on your plate each day. Because, at the surrender of the day, you are in control of what you devour. You can choose to consume in a way that honors your body and your fitness.

Have you ever harassed why there are materials that make you experience actual and others that go away you feeling worn-out and sick? It's no coincidence. Each meals has a unique "energy", a set of homes that have interaction with our organism in a particular way. This is the concept of naturopathic nutrients: information that meals isn't best a group of power, but that it is electricity and lifestyles.

Now, that does not suggest you have to come to be a monk and surrender all of the pleasures of the table. On the opposite, conscious vitamins permits you to experience meals even more, due to the fact you are nourishing your frame in the wonderful viable manner. And you recognize what? There are hundreds of healthy elements which may be delicious. You really should be inclined to find out and strive new matters. Are you organized to preserve this adventure? To discover how nutrients and naturopathy can redesign your life? Then permit's get going!

Secret Herbalism: Plants that Heal

Hello, my pal! Are you organized to embark on any other charming journey on our course to naturopathy? Today, we delve into the mystical worldwide of herbalism. Remember while we talked about the significance of conscious eating in financial disaster 4? How the small choices we make each day ought to have a huge effect on our health and well-being? Well, the electricity of flowers goes even in addition.

But why is herbalism critical? Well, bear in mind being able to deal with a chilly with a cup of chamomile tea in vicinity of a pill. Imagine soothing a burn with sparkling aloe vera in region of a business enterprise cream. Herbalism offers us this possibility.

Of direction, this does not recommend that we need to abandon modern-day treatment. Not in any respect! What naturopathy proposes is an necessary imaginative and prescient of health, in which traditional remedy and herbal restoration procedures art work hand in hand, respecting and taking advantage of the extremely good of each one.

And this is wherein herbal medicinal drug is available in, an ancient paintings that permits us to take gain of the offers that Mother Nature has given us to take care of our health. Surely you apprehend a number of these vegetation. Maybe you operate them in the kitchen, like oregano or rosemary, or maybe you've got got were given them at domestic as ornamental plant life, like lavender or aloe vera. But did you recognize that all of them additionally have powerful recovery houses?

You can be asking yourself, how is it possible that one plant could have such a number of advantages? Well, the answer lies of their chemical composition. Plants produce a big shape of compounds, called phytochemicals, that help them live on and thrive of their herbal environment. Some of those phytochemicals have antibiotic homes, inclusive of these decided in garlic; others are antioxidants, together with those located in berries; others are anti inflammatory, consisting of those observed in turmeric.

Knowing the importance of those inexperienced wonders, it's far essential to say that this isn't always a brand new invention. Plants were on the center of conventional treatment for hundreds of years, and their use is well documented. In historical India, Ayurvedic remedy, which we will talk in Chapter 17, has been based totally on medicinal herbs for more than 5,000 years. Similarly, in historical China, traditional medicinal drug moreover is based closely on herbs and plants. And, of path, indigenous healing practices round the arena have usually included medicinal flowers.

Throughout history, plant experts, which include Paracelsus inside the sixteenth century and Nicholas Culpeper in the seventeenth century, collected a great information of herbalism. Culpeper, in his e-book "The Complete Herbal" posted in 1653, supplied certain descriptions of the houses of loads of flora, maximum of which may be nonetheless used nowadays in present day herbalism.

But what approximately present day-day technology - does it confirm what historical cultures and ancient herbalists have regarded for goodbye? Absolutely. In contemporary years, scientific research has examined most of the medicinal homes of plants that our ancestors knew intuitively. For instance, white willow, which has been used for hundreds of years to deal with pain and fever, consists of a substance known as salicin. Sound familiar? Yes, salicin is the compound this is converted into salicylic acid, the principle aspect of aspirin.

These botanical wonders, the ones real jewels of nature, are there for us. They aren't hidden in a laboratory, nor do they require a PhD to be used. They are surely there, inside the wooded area, within the garden, within the park, looking ahead to us to find out them and consist of them into our each day lives.

But what if I instructed you that a number of the most powerful plants may be on your garden or kitchen right now? What if I counseled you that some basil leaves have to soothe a headache? Or that a cup of peppermint tea may additionally want to help you digest after a heavy meal? What if your little herb garden have to end up your personal private pharmacy? Does that sound exciting? Does that sound thrilling? Does that sound liberating? I do!

Chapter 11: Natural Detoxification

Allow me, my brave fellow vacationer, to inform you a tale that, regardless of the truth that loads of years antique, stays relevant to in recent times. Once upon a time, there has been a glide of easy, glowing water, so lovely that each one the animals of the wooded place came to it to drink. But at some point, the rain introduced with it sediment and debris that clogged its path. The water, as soon as crystal easy, became murky, and the animals stopped coming. However, nature, in her infinite information, delivered a sturdy wind that removed the debris and allowed the water to drift freely all over again. The float regained its clarity and the animals yet again loved its freshness.

And you apprehend what? That move is a metaphor to your frame. Throughout your lifestyles, your frame accumulates pollution, the ones dangerous substances that disrupt its proper functioning, similar to the sediment in the drift. And much like the wind that cleansed the circulation, cleansing is a vital approach to keep the clarity and purity of your body.

But what does it truely suggest to detoxify the frame? And why is it so vital? Detoxification is the approach through which our body removes amassed pollutants. These pollution can come from a whole lot of belongings: the meals we consume, the air we breathe, the chemical compounds we use, or maybe our private metabolic techniques. Now, consider if we should assist our frame in this cleaning manner, take into account the transformation inside the exquisite of your life and properly-being.

Have you ever felt beaten, exhausted, without understanding why? Have you ever felt that however your tremendous efforts, you simply cannot appear to live healthy, irrespective of how hard you strive? Sometimes, that feeling of heaviness and tiredness may be the cease result of a buildup of pollutants in your frame. This is wherein herbal cleansing is available in.

Natural detoxification isn't always a state-of-the-art idea; it is an ancient precept, rooted in plenty of cultures and conventional clinical practices including Ayurveda and traditional Chinese medication. In 2018's "Detoxification: A Clinical Guide," Dr. John B. Sullivan and Gary R. Krieger talk the significance of detoxification and the way our frame has herbal mechanisms to hold it out. However, because of cutting-edge-day life, with its polluted air and water, processed meals and ordinary stress, our body also can need a bit help with this crucial project.

You may be wondering, how can I help my frame on this cleansing tool? Well, there are various procedures to perform that, and at some point of this financial break we will discover numerous of them. But allow me preface this with the useful resource of announcing that the secret's to adopt wholesome and conscious lifestyle behavior, counting on the objects that nature offers us.

Before we embark on our adventure alongside the direction of frame cleansing, I would love you to do a brief exercising of reflection. Remember as quickly as I noted processed foods? How usually every week do you devour this form of meals? And not satisfactory that, how a high-quality deal of these do you consume on a every day foundation? I'm notable you'll be surprised if you knew what number of pollution you will be putting into your body thru your food regimen.

Diet is one of the most identifying factors in the accumulation of pollution. As Dr. Jeffrey Bland cited in his e-book "The Disease Delusion" (2014), regular publicity to processed ingredients, loaded with chemical components and without vital nutrients, can bring about a "toxic funnel" for our frame. But do not worry, the quality news is that it is also the essential problem to assisting our body take away the ones pollution.

This is wherein we need to take a step decrease returned and preserve in thoughts the idea of "aware eating" that we explored in Chapter 4. Mindful eating isn't fine an act of self-love, but additionally an act of cleansing. By choosing natural, chemical-free, nutrient-rich components and ingesting them mindfully, you're supporting your frame do its cleansing art work. Isn't it awesome how these kind of portions healthful collectively?

Now, beyond diet, there are numerous unique strategies you could help your body in this cleaning system. For instance, fasting, practiced on the grounds that time immemorial in plenty of cultures, is a effective detoxification device. During a short, you deliver your body a damage from digestion, permitting it to pay interest its efforts on eliminating pollution.

But a manner to put into effect fasting efficiently and successfully? According to Dr. Alan Goldhamer and Dr. Jennifer Marano in their e-book "The Health Promoting

Cookbook" (1997), fasting should be completed carefully and continuously with the useful resource of a health professional who can manual you through the device. And that is some issue I want to emphasize: any massive exchange in your food plan or way of life must normally be finished under the steerage of a fitness professional.

At this thing, I need you to understand that herbal detoxification is a adventure, not a destination. It is a regular exercise, a healthy dependancy which you need to include into your manner of life. It isn't always some thing you do as soon as and overlook approximately about, but some component you do regularly to preserve readability and purity for your body.

But what if I informed you that there is a manner to assist your body in this cleansing gadget at the equal time as you sleep? Yes, you examine that proper. In the following segment, we can explore how the great of your sleep might also have an effect to your potential to detoxify your body. So, are you ready to maintain on this wonderful journey of cleaning?

Well, permit me assist you to realize a hint extra approximately this remarkable nocturnal device. While you sleep, your mind performs a shape of "residence cleaning". The lymphatic gadget, a community of vessels that run in a few unspecified time in the future of your body removing waste, is also placed on your mind. However, this mind lymphatic machine has a completely unique call: the glymphatic gadget. In their 2013 check, "Sleep Drives Metabolite Clearance from the Adult Brain," Dr. Maiken Nedergaard and co-workers determined that this glymphatic gadget is especially energetic within the route of sleep. Therefore, first rate sleep allows for greater powerful brain cleansing.

However, records how this nocturnal cleansing takes location is not sufficient. You moreover need to recognise how you may have an effect on this machine. One of the simplest techniques is to installation a healthful sleep routine. You recognize, the ones topics your grandmother used to inform you approximately going to mattress early and getting up with the sun. As it seems, she modified into so right.

Mindfulness and Meditation: Calming the Mind to Heal the Body

I'm first rate you have found yourself inside the middle of a worrying state of affairs, right? Maybe you have got got been stuck in website website traffic, with time pressing and an crucial dedication you could not be past due for. Did you feel your respiration quicken, anxiety assemble on your shoulders, and your stomach knot up? If the answer is yes, then you have professional firsthand how the thoughts can have an effect on the frame.

Now, lets say that you may alternate your reaction to these situations. Imagine that, in desire to permitting strain to control you, you could stay calm, attention at the triumphing, and one manner or the alternative melt that bodily reaction. Sound now not feasible? Well, permit me display you the manner the practice of mindfulness and meditation can accomplish exactly that.

You want to bear in thoughts that we are whole beings. If you reflect onconsideration on it, the thoughts and body are intrinsically connected entities which have an effect on every unique in big methods, and this is a concept that naturopathy respects and encourages. Thus, if we need to discover a extra natural course to pinnacle of the road health, it's miles vital that we delve into the terrific courting between mind and body.

Mindfulness and meditation have been practiced for loads of years in numerous cultures and traditions. But what are they in truth and the way can they assist us heal and live a greater in shape, greater enriching existence?

Mindfulness" is a phrase this is often translated as "mindfulness" or "aware popularity". It is a exercising of intentionally listening to what's going on within the gift, with out judgment. In this manner, you grow to be an observer of your mind, emotions, and physical sensations, in choice to automatically reacting to them.

Meditation, however, is a exercising that regularly consists of the usage of mindfulness, but may be extra installed. There are numerous forms of meditation, from awareness meditation, which includes that specialize in a unmarried trouble, to coronary coronary heart-starting meditation, which incorporates cultivating emotions of kindness and compassion.

Now, have you ever ever puzzled how the clean movement of that specialize inside the gift and your non-public internal opinions could have this form of profound impact for your health and properly-being? Well, you'll be surprised to study that there may be a huge quantity of studies supporting the benefits of mindfulness and meditation.

According to Professor Jon Kabat-Zinn, founder of the Mindfulness-Based Stress Reduction (MBSR) software program on the University of Massachusetts, in his ebook "Full Catastrophe Living" (1990), mindfulness and meditation practices can assist reduce pressure and tension, enhance focus and reminiscence, and promote a more feel of properly-being and pleasure in existence. Surprising, is not it? But it in reality is clearly the begin.

Imagine for a second which you are in a wooded area. Birdsong fills the air, and a slight breeze rustles thru the leaves of the wood. You enjoy the freshness of the air to your pores and skin and the fragrance of damp earth. You comprehend that, rather than considering what you need to do later or disturbing about what came about the day before today, you are honestly present, clearly immersed within the "right here and now". This is the essence of mindfulness.

Dr. Herbert Benson, writer of "The Relaxation Response" (1975), documented how meditation can counteract the consequences of the so-called "fight or flight reflex," that is activated in worrying conditions. By activating a "relaxation reaction," meditation can reduce coronary heart charge, lower blood stress and reduce the manufacturing of cortisol, a pressure-associated hormone. This trade in physiological response can be very beneficial, specially while we stay in this sort of demanding, stress-crammed society.

Remember whilst we pointed out the significance of stability in monetary damage 3? Well, mindfulness and meditation can be powerful tools to restore that balance and help us higher control stress and tension in our each day lives.

But how do you workout mindfulness and meditation? Although they may appear like summary or maybe intimidating ideas, the reality is that the ones are easy techniques which can be available to each person.

To exercising mindfulness, you really need to pick out out a time of the day and decide to pay entire interest to what is taking region at that 2nd. It may be at the same time as brushing your tooth, even as eating, or maybe while respiration. Pay hobby to the sensations on your frame, to the sounds round you, to the mind that stand up on your thoughts. Observe it all without judgment, in truth permitting your self to be within the present.

Meditation, as a substitute, may additionally moreover require a piece greater form. You can start with the aid of selecting a quiet place with out a distractions, and set apart a few minutes every day on your exercise. You can also select to focus in your respiratory, on a word or word (known as a mantra), or on feelings of love and kindness for your self and others.

Like any ability, the practice of mindfulness and meditation calls for time and determination. Don't despair if in advance than the whole thing you find out it difficult to preserve your attention inside the present or to calm your mind. Remember, it's far now not approximately accomplishing a nation of splendid rest or having no mind, but approximately growing a greater aware and moderate courting collectively together with your very private mind and frame.

So, what do you're saying, are you equipped to embark in this thrilling course to intellectual calm and bodily restoration? Remember, on this adventure you aren't by myself. I am right here with you, guiding you grade by grade. And accept as true with me, the journey is well really worth it.

Chapter 12: Its Role In Naturopathy

My high priced reader, you can have observed that during our adventure via the wonders of naturopathy, we are often called to move lower back to the basics, to the most important elements of lifestyles, to that which gives existence and sustains our life. Well, nowadays is not any exception. Today, we delve into the depths of a crucial detail, one which covers greater than 70% of our planet and makes up about the identical percentage of our frame. Today, we talk approximately water, the elixir of life.

As you observe this, you are probably asking yourself, what can be so specific about water? Isn't it virtually a tasteless, odorless, colorless liquid that we drink to quench our thirst? Let me allow you to know, expensive reader, that water is much more than that. It is an detail as charming as it is important to our fitness and properly-being. So, will you be part of me in this adventure to find out the magic of water and its relevance to naturopathy?

Water is, simply, the most treasured beneficial resource we've were given. Without it, life as we understand it may clearly now not be feasible. In the vicinity of fitness, water performs an crucial characteristic. It lets in us live hydrated, regulate our body temperature, lubricate our joints and important organs, shipping vitamins to our cells and flush pollutants from our our our bodies, amongst many precise capabilities. It is, in brief, the fuel that feeds and keeps our organic equipment walking.

Have you ever belief approximately what a miracle it's far that we are composed greater frequently than no longer of water? Have you ever contemplated on how water, this kind of easy and considerable element, may have this type of profound effect on our fitness and properly-being? I invite you to take a second to accomplish that, because of the truth appreciating the significance of water in our lives is the first step to information its characteristic in naturopathy.

Naturopathy, as we've already mentioned in previous chapters, is based totally totally on the idea that the body has the inherent capability to heal itself, as extended because it is provided with what it wants to reap this. And water, luxurious reader, is the sort of important elements that our body wishes to live healthy and feature nicely.

However, it is vital to be conscious that no longer all water is the identical. The terrific of the water we eat may also need to have a exquisite impact on our health. In the subsequent phase of this financial ruin, we are able to discover this subject matter in addition, delving into the generation of water and its exceptional workplace work. I will introduce you to the findings of numerous distinguished authors on this challenge, together with Dr. Masaru Emoto, author of "The Hidden Messages in Water" (2004), who committed his life to analyzing the molecular shape of water and the manner it could be inspired with the beneficial resource of factors in conjunction with human emotions, thoughts and phrases.

So, as we dive deeper into this captivating global of water, I invite you to take a look at a glass of water with a selected eye. Is it in reality water, or is there an entire universe of opportunities hidden in every drop? Are you ready to dive deeper into this mysterious watery world with me?

The water we drink, use for cooking and bathing is not certainly H2O. It is a wealthy medium that consists of minerals, vitamins and, regrettably in many areas, contaminants. Hence, water purity has turn out to be a critical health problem in our instances.

And that is where the art work of Dr. Masaru Emoto will become relevant. This Japanese researcher amazed the arena together together with his snap shots of frozen water crystals. By exposing water to at least one-of-a-kind phrases, mind, kinds of song and prayers, he decided that the water "spoke back" to the ones influences via changing its crystalline shape. Words and thoughts of love and gratitude created stunning, symmetrical crystals, while awful phrases and thoughts produced distorted crystals.

Now, you could ask, what does all this mean for us? How does it relate to naturopathy and our health? Well, if mind, terms and feelings can trade the form of water, and our frame is in maximum instances composed of water, isn't it viable that our thoughts, phrases and feelings actually have a right away impact on our fitness and well-being?

This line of idea isn't always new. As early as 1936, Dr. Alexis Carrel, Nobel Laureate in Medicine, said in his e-book "Man, The Unknown" that human thoughts and emotions have a right away impact on the health of the frame. If we extrapolate this to the water in our our our bodies, we're able to begin to glimpse the depth of the results.

So what are you able to, my steeply-priced reader, do with this statistics? You might also additionally want to begin thru manner of listening to the superb of the water you eat. Is it natural? Is it free of contaminants? In addition, you could begin experimenting collectively along with your private mind and emotions. Remember the terms of gratitude and love that Emoto used in his experiments and strive infusing your water with high-quality thoughts in advance than you drink it. Do you phrase any difference in the manner you feel?

The Sun and Us: How Natural Light Affects Us

I advocate that, for a 2d, you close up your eyes and reflect onconsideration on a sunny day. Can you sense the first-rate and comfortable mild piercing your eyelids and spilling over your pores and skin? Can you perceive that clean stimulus that gives you energy and makes you revel in lively and full of strength?

The sun, that exquisite sparkling sphere inside the sky, has been worshipped in ancient cultures, the scenario of legends and songs, and continues to be an inexhaustible deliver of life. Now, ask yourself: How usually an afternoon do you truely feel the sun on your pores and pores and skin? Have you ever stopped to reflect onconsideration on the effect that herbal moderate has to your existence and your fitness?

The energy of natural light, especially daylight hours, is regularly underestimated. However, each ray of sunlight hours that touches our skin triggers a cascade of occasions in our body, from the manufacturing of nutrition D to the law of our circadian rhythms, the internal clocks that manage our sleep and wake patterns. Throughout this chapter, we are able to discover the ones methods huge and discover the manner to maximize the blessings of daylight hours at the same time as averting its capability risks.

To start, permit's communicate approximately a bit hormone you've got probably heard of earlier than: vitamins D. Despite its call, nutrition D is honestly a hormone that our body produces while our pores and pores and skin is exposed to daylight. It is vital for a number of natural functions, from calcium absorption and bone fitness, to modulating the immune system.

But right right here's the thrilling detail: regular with the World Health Organization, a huge percent of the area's populace is deficient in nutrients D. Does that sound sudden? I actually have grow to be amazed before everything, too. In a worldwide wherein the sun shines on us every day, how is it feasible that so lots folks lack this essential weight loss plan?

The answer lies in our modern-day behavior and lifestyles. Most folks spend most of our day interior, whether or not going for walks in an place of work, studying in a university or enjoyable at home. Direct daylight hours not often touches our skin. And even because it does, we're often protected with the resource of manner of layers of sunscreen that block weight loss plan D production.

Don't get me incorrect, solar safety is important to prevent pores and pores and skin harm and pores and skin most cancers. However, it's also vital that we find a wholesome balance amongst defensive our pores and pores and pores and skin and allowing our body to provide the weight loss program D it dreams.

In this regard, you could have heard of the "noon sun" rule proposed by means of using Michael F. Holick, in his ebook "The Vitamin D Solution" (2010). Holick shows that sun publicity of 10 to 1/2-hour on the face, arms and palms with out sunscreen, at least times every week, can provide the important ranges of vitamins D. However, by no means all through the hours of maximum sun radiation and continually counting on your pores and skin type and geographical place.

But now you'll be questioning, why is vitamins D so important? This hormone is a pillar for bone fitness and the immune device, as we already stated, but there can be more.

According to research at the side of the simplest through Grant, Garland and Holick in 2005, weight loss plan D may additionally have a defensive characteristic in preventing tremendous types of cancer, coronary coronary heart ailment and autoimmune issues, amongst others.

And right here's a few different element: our mood. Have you ever found how a sunny day can beautify your spirits, on the same time as a cloudy day could make you revel in a touch down? That's no longer best a perception Sunlight surely has an impact on our mood and emotional well-being.

This is due to the fact publicity to daylight affects the producing of serotonin, a neurotransmitter this is related to mood and well-being. Have you heard of seasonal affective illness (SAD)? It is a form of despair that takes place in a few people inside the course of the autumn and iciness months, at the same time as sunlight hours is shorter. Studies, which embody one finished with the resource of Rosenthal et al. In 1984, have recommended that slight treatments can also assist alleviate SAD signs and signs and symptoms through manner of growing serotonin production.

In addition, sunlight hours moreover impacts the producing of melatonin, the hormone that allows us sleep. When the solar is going down and mild decreases, our frame produces more melatonin, getting prepared us for relaxation. Conversely, on the identical time because the solar rises and the moderate will increase, melatonin manufacturing decreases, signaling that it is time to evoke.

We must bypass on and on approximately the blessings of daylight hours. But do no longer you discovered we sometimes forget about about how tremendous this natural beneficial resource is? In our modern lives, in which generation and homes sometimes separate us from the herbal worldwide, it is able to be clean to forget how heaps we rely on daylight for our properly-being.

So I encourage you to do not forget how you could consist of more daytime into your lifestyles in a healthful way. Do you have a place in your own home wherein lots of natural slight is to be had in? Could you set up your day so that you can flow for a walk whilst the solar is shining?

Remember, it's miles constantly essential to shield your pores and skin. It's not approximately irresponsible solar exposure, but about locating a wholesome stability that permits your frame to gain from sunlight hours at the equal time as protective your pores and pores and skin from harm.

Chapter 13: Sleep And Restoration

Welcome lower lower back, my steeply-priced reader, have you ever ever had a tiring day? How approximately a plan? Let me take you on a adventure into the area of sleep, wherein we are able to observe collectively how proper rest can repair and rejuvenate our mind and frame.

Have you ever puzzled why we want sleep? Well, it's miles some thing that technology remains exploring - are you able to take shipping of as genuine with it? Something that every and every one parents does, every day of our lives, remains shrouded in mystery. But right here's what we do recognize: sleep is not a steeply-priced, but a want. It is as important to our well-being as eating or breathing.

Now, why is sleep so important? For starters, it's far a time of repair and restoration for our frame and mind. While we sleep, our body goes to paintings on preservation duties that it can't carry out during our waking hours. It upkeep muscles, regenerates cells and consolidates our recollections, in reality to call a number of its competencies.

Have you noticed how after an extraordinary night time's sleep you enjoy rejuvenated, complete of energy and optimism? That's due to the fact sleep furthermore influences our temper and emotional nicely-being. Conversely, loss of sleep can bring about irritability, lack of expertise or maybe long-time period fitness issues which includes coronary heart illness, diabetes and despair

So what happens if we do not get sufficient sleep or if the extremely good of our sleep isn't always the superb? Have you ever had that feeling of highbrow exhaustion, loss of popularity, an irritable temper after a night time time of interrupted or inadequate sleep? That's proof of the crucial function sleep plays in our lives.

So certain, expensive reader, sleep is critical. And no, it isn't time wasted. Rather, it is time nicely spent, a present we supply ourselves to be greater wholesome, more focused and happier.

Yet no matter all this, in our contemporary, annoying society, sleep is frequently the primary to be sacrificed. How normally have you ever heard or maybe said yourself, "I'll sleep as soon as I'm useless"? That kind of mentality is what leads us to despise sleep, to maintain in mind it a waste of time in place of the precious investment it truely is.

In this bankruptcy, we are going to exchange that. I'm going to guide you through the technology of sleep, the way it impacts our frame and thoughts, and the way we are able to enhance the quality of our sleep. Are you prepared to join me on this adventure via the geographical areas of Morpheus? Are you prepared to analyze the way nicely sleep can repair your frame, enhance your highbrow fitness, and increase your energy and energy? Then allow's get comfortable, placed our troubles aside for now, and find out the mysterious global of sleep.

Think about your fashionable sleep sample. Do you locate it clean to fall into the hands of Morpheus every night time time? Or are you considered honestly one in every of those who toss and turn in mattress, gazing the darkish ceiling? You are not by myself, expensive reader, if the latter satisfactory describes you. Matthew Walker, in his ebook "Why We Sleep" (2017), shows that up to two-thirds of adults in advanced international locations do now not get the amount of sleep endorsed via the World Health Organization. Can you believe?

The Essence of Movement: The Role of Exercise in Natural Health

Movement, my friend, is a lot greater than moving from one area to every different. Movement is existence. Imagine for a second which you are a tree. You have roots that penetrate deep into the earth, a sturdy trunk that holds you upright, and branches that acquire in the direction of the sky. Although you appear motionless, you're in normal movement. Sap flows through you, sporting nutrients and water from the roots to the very great leaves. Your leaves capture daytime and convert that strength into meals. Even your branches and leaves circulate with the wind, adapting to converting conditions.

Now, bypass decrease returned to being yourself. Even even though you are sitting here analyzing this ebook, your frame is also in regular motion. Blood flows via your veins and arteries, carrying oxygen and nutrients to each cellular for your frame. Your lungs make bigger and settlement with each breath, converting carbon dioxide for oxygen. Your muscle tissue and tendons modify and realign with even the slightest trade in your posture. Even whilst you sleep, your mind continues to characteristic, processing the day's data and getting prepared you for what lies in advance.

So why can we want to workout? Well, permit me ask you every one-of-a-kind query: have you ever ever ever had a garden or potted plant? If so, then you definitely recognize that the plant needs extra than sincerely water and daytime to thrive. It desires the right soil, likely a chunk fertilizer and it certainly desires to be pruned sometimes to preserve its maximum green shape and health.

Similarly, our our bodies want greater than certainly meals and relaxation to thrive. We need the proper motion, probable a hint "fertilizer" within the form of active workout, and we actually need to be "pruned" every so often, to preserve our muscle companies and joints in well shape. And no, I'm now not suggesting you want to take pruning shears to it, sincerely that normal exercise will assist you to preserve a healthy stability of energy and flexibility, in addition to improve waft and cardiovascular health.

A few centuries in the past, our ancestors did not want to go to the gymnasium to workout. Their active life furnished all the motion they needed. But within the modern technology, an entire lot of us spend most of our day sitting within the the front of a table, pc show or television. As a give up end result, our our bodies crave and want movement greater than ever.

No depend how active or inactive you have got were given been thus far, there may be always room for improvement. So in this monetary smash, we are going to discover a few methods you may incorporate extra movement into your lifestyles in a manner it virtually is exciting and sustainable for you.

Will you be part of this dance of movement, this waltz of lifestyles, wherein your body is the protagonist and each step is a be conscious inside the music of your fitness and properly-being? I promise you, it is going to be a charming dance.

Now, allow's reflect onconsideration on the unique styles of movement you may include into your life. To do that, I would like to cite Frank Forencich, author of "The Exuberant Animal: The Power of Health, Play and Joyful Movement" (2006). In his ebook, Forencich explores the one-of-a-kind forms of motion that our ancestors practiced on a daily basis and the way we're capable of include them into our current lives. He says, and I quote, "We are not simply our bodies that want to move to burn electricity. We are exuberant animals that thrive on the pride and a laugh of motion."

The first shape of movement Forencich mentions is straightforward movement for survival. In historical instances, this covered looking, amassing food, constructing refuge and protecting oneself from predators. Today, this may translate to strolling to the grocery preserve, wearing grocery luggage domestic, or mountaineering stairs instead of taking the elevator. Do you realise how those small, regular sports activities are truely varieties of movement that make contributions for your health?

The 2d kind of motion is play. Yes, you heard right, play. Remember at the same time as you were a toddler and you could spend hours playing outdoors, strolling, jumping, mountaineering? As adults, we often forget about about the rate of play, however it is however a important part of our well-being. Not notable does play allow us to move our bodies in numerous and hard strategies, but it moreover nourishes our minds and spirits. So why no longer set up a pastime of football with pals or an afternoon of hiking in nature?

The zero.33 form of motion is dance. And no, you do not should be a professional dancer to enjoy the blessings of dance. Dance is a form of expression that includes rhythm, track, and creativity, and can be a great way to transport your body. And do not forget, you can moreover dance within the privacy of your property, to your preferred tune.

The remaining sort of movement that Forencich highlights is ritual. This is a type of movement with a purpose or because of this past the bodily activity itself. Think of the postures in a yoga elegance, the moves of a martial paintings, or even the gestures carried out in a religious ceremony.

These 4 types of movement, number one, play, dance and ritual, provide us a range of alternatives for incorporating movement into our lives in a manner that aligns with our pastimes, abilities and desires.

But let me ask you, whilst modified into the remaining time you moved in a way that without a doubt made you enjoy alive, critical, and complete of joy? If you can not take into account, probable it is time to rethink how you can add extra movement to your life. And bear in mind, each step you're taking is a step in the direction of more colourful fitness and a happier life. Are you equipped to preserve dancing with me in this adventure closer to fitness and well-being thru movement?

Sure, permit's keep dancing together on this charming dance of movement. To that surrender, let's have a look at some concrete examples of methods you could consist of greater motion into your life, regardless of your current health diploma.

Let's start with the essential movement. This is the form of movement that you may comprise into your every day ordinary with out even figuring out it. For example, you could determine to get off the bus one save you early and walk the rest of the manner domestic. Or you could begin making small changes at home, inclusive of having up and moving in the course of enterprise breaks while you are looking TV or setting a reminder to stand up and stretch every hour if you work sitting down.

I stated Frank Forencich above, however I additionally need to cite Katy Bowman, author of "Move Your DNA: Restore Your Health Through Natural Movement" (2014). Bowman argues that even the smallest, reputedly insignificant movements should have a profound impact on our health and properly-being. She writes, "It's now not without a doubt the quantity of motion that topics, however furthermore the nice and kind of that movement."

Remember the idea of the sport we cited in advance? Gaming is not only for youngsters, and it is in no manner too overdue to begin gambling all yet again. You must be a part of up for a recreational sports activities team, like soccer, basketball, or even remaining frisbee. Or you could try some component new, like mountaineering, surfing, or kayaking. The aim isn't always to end up an elite athlete, but to learn how to pass that make you revel in alive and whole of satisfaction.

Dance is each other tremendous way to move the frame in severa and difficult tactics. There are such a whole lot of kinds of dance to explore, from salsa and tango to hip-hop and cutting-edge dance. It could not depend in case you experience awkward or in case you assume you have no rhythm. Dance is not approximately being best, it's miles about expressing yourself and gambling the motion.

And in the end, there can be ritual movement, the kind this is going past the physical interest itself. If you have got been considering trying yoga, tai chi or some form of martial artwork, now is probably the time. These forms of movement will not exceptional help you're making stronger your frame, but may additionally even help you cultivate interest, staying energy, and intellectual and emotional stability.

I invite you to check, to find out, to have amusing. Movement is a top notch present, and every of us has the potential to transport in strategies that could nurture our health and properly-being. So what do you say, are you prepared to embark in this journey, to find out the exceptional methods you can circulate and characteristic fun your frame?

Chapter 14: The Vibration Of Music

Have you ever felt a shiver run down your spine while you are taking note of a bit of track that movements you? Have you ever felt how a unhappy song pushes you to shed tears, or how a glad melody fills you with strength and optimism? That, expensive reader, is the strength of music, a regular artwork that deeply impacts our feelings, our mind and, yes, also our fitness.

Music, that wonderful mixture of rhythm, melody and concord, has a very unique characteristic in our lives. It is a form of deep conversation this is going past phrases and can connect us with our inner most emotions, with our maximum forgotten reminiscences, and with that part of us this is pure essence, natural vibration.

Throughout the centuries, song has been a crucial a part of the celebrations, rituals and ceremonies of in fact each way of life in the global. But why is it so important? What is it about song that affects us so profoundly? The answer lies in vibration.

Yes, my buddy, the entirety in this universe vibrates, from the smallest subatomic debris to the most vital galaxies. And we, people, also are vibrational beings. Our body, our organs, our cells, they all vibrate at their very own frequency. And this is wherein music comes into play.

Music is vibration and, on the identical time because it interacts with us, it may effect our very own vibrations. This is how a song must make us experience unhappy or happy, relaxed or excited. But it is going similarly: with the useful resource of affecting our vibrations, track can also have a profound impact on our bodily and highbrow properly-being.

That's why in recent times, in this bankruptcy, we can embark on an thrilling journey via the universe of tune and its recovery power. We will see how precise styles of music may want to have an impact on our health, how tune remedy is being used to help people overcome all varieties of fitness issues and the manner you can use song on your each day lifestyles to enhance your well-being.

Are you organized to discover the magic of melodies and vibrations? Are you organized to find out how a easy track can trade your temper, relieve your pressure, and even assist you heal? If so, music your ears, open your coronary coronary heart and get prepared for the incredible symphony of recovery thru track.

In this exciting adventure thru harmonies and melodies, I invite you to recollect something you cannot have notion of before. I advocate you to see music not only as a form of enjoyment or a device to precise your feelings, but additionally as a shape of medication. Yes, you test that right, song may be a clearly effective treatment, able to recovery every the body and the thoughts.

Sound extraordinary? Let me introduce you to someone who has devoted his lifestyles to proving it. I'm speaking about Oliver Sacks, a celebrated neurologist and author, recognized for his precise research at the outcomes of song on the human mind. In his e-book "Musicophilia" (2007), Sacks determined out how song might also have a profound effect on our brains, even the ones broken with the useful resource of ailment or damage.

Sacks tells recollections of human beings with aphasia, a condition that prevents them from processing language, but who can however sing and recognize songs. He tells of people with Parkinson's contamination who, no matter the fact that they have got hassle transferring, can dance consequences to the beat of a music. And there are testimonies of people with Alzheimer's, who cannot remember their cherished ones, however can despite the fact that maintain in thoughts and sing the songs of their young adults.

How is that this possible? Sacks described that track can get right of entry to components of the brain that unique kinds of communique can't. When we pay attention to tune, we spark off areas of our brain associated with motion, emotion, reminiscence and reward. And while we play an instrument, even more areas are activated, which includes those associated with incredible motor coordination, being attentive to and imaginative and prescient.

But it isn't first rate scientists and neurologists who recognize the recuperation electricity of music. Indigenous peoples round the place have used tune and track as a vital part of their restoration practices for lots of years. For them, music is a device to connect to the spirit, to invoke the help of the gods, to purify the frame and thoughts, and to unite the community in times of disaster.

A specially captivating example of this is located most of the Suya, an indigenous tribe in Brazil. According to anthropologist Anthony Seeger in his e book "Why Suya Sing" (1987), the Suya accept as genuine with that making a song is crucial for specific fitness and well-being. They obtain as genuine with that singing can therapy ailments, enhance the frame and guard in competition to evil spirits.

So, expensive reader, with all this in mind, I ask you: How are you the use of music to your lifestyles? Are you aware of how the music you pick out to pay attention to can affect your fitness and nicely-being? Are you willing to discover new methods to consist of track into your existence to beautify your fitness? Remember, music is not actually enjoyment, it could be your incredible friend, your treatment, your direction to extra health and properly being. And that is truly the begin of our musical journey.

So, now that we agree that track has wonderful electricity to heal, how are you going to exquisite harness it? Let me offer you with a few realistic tips.

To start with, remember that music might be very personal. What may be a chilled melody to as a minimum one character can be a cacophony to another. The secret is to listen to what really resonates with you, makes you glad, calms you, or motivates you, counting on what your want is at the time. There is not any single "recipe" that works for all and sundry; as a substitute, it is a journey of musical self-discovery.

You may surprise if there are certain sorts of song which can be more recovery than others. According to investigate, classical tune, in particular, has been tested to have severa fitness advantages, from lowering blood strain and pressure to improving sleep and temper. A 2013 take a look at published inside the mag Trends in Cognitive Sciences showed that listening to classical track, specifically Mozart and Strauss, induced huge decreases in blood strain and coronary heart charge.

Chapter 15: The Healing Power Of Smells

Let me ask you a question, have you ever walked down a road and caught a whiff of a acquainted perfume that right now transported you to a memory from the past? Perhaps the aroma of your grandmother's freshly baked cookies, or the perfume of freshly lessen grass on a heat summer season day. How did that make you feel? Did you take a look at how that perfume had the capability to evoke immoderate emotions, to take you to a completely special vicinity and time within the blink of a watch constant constant? If so, then you definitely've already skilled the strength of aromatherapy.

Aromas have an exquisite capability to persuade our psyche, and their use in recuperation dates lower lower back to historical instances. The Egyptians, for example, used fragrant oils for their embalming practices, recognizing their capacity to maintain and purify. But did you understand that the ones aromas can also have a profound impact on our health and nicely-being?

Aromatherapy, as it's miles seemed nowadays, refers back to the restoration use of important oils extracted from plant life, plant life, herbs and spices. Each of those oils has a completely precise aroma profile and precise healing houses. When inhaled or absorbed thru the pores and pores and pores and skin, they might have an effect on our emotions, relieve strain, decorate mood, promote extraordinary sleep, and offer some of fitness benefits.

While it's miles real that the effects of smells can range from character to character, have you ever ever ever noticed that certain smells have the capability to steer your temper in a comparable way every time you enjoy them? This is because of the close to relationship among our feel of heady scent and our limbic gadget, the center of our feelings inside the thoughts.

Robert Tisserand, one of the most renowned specialists within the situation of aromatherapy, explains it masterfully in his e-book "The Art of Aromatherapy" (1977). According to him, "When we inhale the aroma of an critical oil, it's far transported through our nose to the olfactory bulb, in which the messages are transmitted to the limbic gadget. From there, they may be able to have an effect on emotions, behaviors or maybe bodily functions at the side of coronary heart charge and blood pressure."

As we pass beforehand in this economic damage, we're capable of invite you to open your senses and your mind to the olfactory global. Let's discover together how vital oils may be effective machine for restoration and nicely being, learn how to use them well and efficaciously, and explore how those fantastic gadgets of nature will permit you to in your adventure to top-rated health. Are you organized to embark on this aromatic journey with me? If your answer is yes, then allow's take a deep breath and get commenced.

In the second one 1/2 of of the 20th century, Marguerite Maury, a French nurse, brought the idea of using essential oils on an individualized basis, tailor-made to the specific desires of all of us. In her seminal ebook "The Secret of Life and Youth" (1964), Maury argued that aromatherapy can be masses more than actually a way to alleviate physical symptoms. She endorsed the concept that, by using the use of thinking about the individuality of the character, important oils can be a effective device for prevention and properly being.

I actually have usually been curious approximately the concept that with the aid of hook or with the aid of criminal our nose is aware of greater about us than our personal aware mind. You may be asking your self, how is that feasible? Well, consider it, have you ever ever ever felt an instinctive repulsion closer to a odor that others locate extraordinary? Or have you ever ever determined your self loving a perfume that others discover unpleasant? That's your nose, dialoguing right away with your brain, your feelings, your personal statistics.

And, yes, it is viable that a number of the answers to these puzzles lie in our genetics. As Patricia Davis factors out in her ebook "Aromatherapy: An A-Z" (1988), our genes ought to have an impact on our olfactory options. That's why a few smells entice us at the same time as others repel us.

Now, before we get into the nitty-gritty of the manner aromatherapy can improve our lives, I need to ensure we understand one factor. Aromatherapy is extra than just smelling proper. While it's miles real that great aromas can beautify our mood, the recovery blessings of critical oils skip past virtually a pleasant perfume.

You can also wonder, then, how can we harness the strength of scents in our each day lives? How can important oils assist us beautify our nicely-being and live a more healthy existence? Well, my buddy, permit's hold exploring together, diving deeper into the ocean of scents and their mysteries.

And earlier than we hold, I want to remind you, typically with a smile, that vital oils are very strong concentrates, so please keep in thoughts that it's far critical to use them accurately. So please hold in thoughts that it is important to use them successfully. Now, permit's get into the captivating global of aromatherapy! Are you equipped to preserve this journey with me? Here we flow into!

Here we are, going deeper into the heart of aromatherapy! Are you gambling the adventure? Can you already experience your information spreading like a perfume inside the air? Let's circulate on.

Imagine coming home after an prolonged day at art work. You experience the weight of the hours piling up to your shoulders. Perhaps your mind continues to be twisted up inside the problems and demanding situations of the day. What have to you do to change that electricity? This is where aromatherapy can paintings its magic.

You take a small bottle of lavender essential oil, a plant loved for its easy and soothing perfume. Gingerly, you pour some drops into your diffuser and flip it on. Gradually, the fragrance of lavender starts offevolved offevolved to permeate the air. Your shoulders begin to loosen up, your agitated thoughts start to calm. That's aromatherapy in movement.

But why does this take place, and the manner can a easy scent spark off this form of alternate in our mood and physical nicely-being? According to Kurt Schnaubelt in his ebook "Advanced Aromatherapy" (1998), critical oils incorporate chemical compounds that interact with our frame at numerous degrees. For example, lavender oil consists of linalool, a compound that has calming outcomes at the nervous device. And so, via inhaling lavender oil, we are permitting the linalool to act on our frame.

www.ingramcontent.com/pod-product-compliance
Lightning Source LLC
Chambersburg PA
CBHW071620030726
47598CB00001B/365